# EASY LIONEL LAYOUTS YOU CAN BUILD

Peter H. Riddle

KALMBACH
BOOKS

Printed in the United States of America

97 98 99 00 01 02 03 04 05 06    10 9 8 7 6 5 4 3 2 1

For more information, visit our website at
http://www.kalmbach.com

Publisher's Cataloging-in-Publication
(Provided by Quality Books, Inc.)

Riddle, Peter.
Easy Lionel layouts you can build : 29 new designs / Peter H. Riddle. — 1st ed.
p.  cm.
Includes bibliographical references.

1. Railroads—Models. 2. Lionel Corporation. I. Title.

TF197.R49 1997                          625.1'9
                                              QBI97-40476

Book design: Jennifer Gaertner
Cover design: Kristi Ludwig

The author would like to thank Gay Riddle and Roger Carp for their editing.

# CONTENTS

# DEDICATION

This book owes its existence in part to my wife's mom and dad and is dedicated to them with gratitude and love: Gertrude Anne Bull, whose home currently shelters my Standard gauge layout, and the late Harold M. Bull, whose gift to me of his boyhood Ives clockwork set rekindled my interest in old toy trains.

# 1

## INTRODUCTION

Beginning as early as 1922 and continuing today, most of the colorful catalogs published by Lionel have included one or more pages of layout designs. While their main purpose undoubtedly was to promote the sale of extra track, turnouts (Lionel calls them "switches"), and crossovers, these layout plan suggestions also served to stimulate the imagination of operators, opening their eyes to the possibilities of creating one's own railroad empire.

The earlier designs tend to be symmetrical and to favor continuous running on loops of track. In later years, as Lionel introduced remote-control reversing and uncoupling, as well as a variety of clever operating cars, layout designers added reverse loops and sidings. With the advent of Magne-Traction in the early 1950s, bilevel plans soon appeared in the instruction books that came packed with every train set. In a section of these books entitled "How to Build a Model Railroad," Lionel promoted the sale of its track, trestles, and accessories by showing attractive possibilities for their use.

Most of these published track plans are well conceived and, if reproduced exactly, produce satisfying, trouble-free model railroads. You may, however, realize a greater sense of achievement through creating a unique, individualized layout that reflects your own preferences and operating style. This book is designed to get you started on building just such a personalized empire, first by helping you discover what kind of a layout will satisfy you best and then by offering sample plans that you can copy directly or expand on and adapt to your individual needs.

You will find that I have included no designs to fill an attic or basement. Many model railroaders may dream of building and owning such a railroad empire, but the realities of contemporary life dictate that the majority of toy train enthusiasts have only a limited amount of space they can divert from other household needs and devote to the hobby.

In many respects, building a large layout places fewer demands upon a modeler's creativity and ingenuity than

building a small one. When a large amount of space is available, you can include multiple main lines and numerous sidings and accessories with ease. By contrast, finding ways to pack lasting interest into a layout that has room for only modest amounts of track, scenery, and accessories will seriously tax your imagination.

Each of the layouts featured in this book can fit easily in a spare room, and many can be contained within an unused corner of a den or bedroom. Beginners should find them approachable; experienced modelers will find enough challenges to exercise their creativity with sophisticated wiring and highly realistic scenery. The emphasis of each design is an interesting track plan combined with the maximum amount of operating possibilities. You can build any or all of these using inexpensive and readily available sectional track.

### TRACK PRODUCTS

There are many different track products available on today's market, ranging from the time-tested and familiar sectional toy train track to more realistic flexible rails mounted on closely spaced wooden ties. Lionel's sectional track is the easiest to use, but its tubular rails and widely spaced metal ties hardly resemble the real

Fig. 1-1. GarGraves flexible track offers several significant advantages over sectional track when used on permanent layouts: realistic appearance, infinitely variable curve radii, and inherent adaptability to accessory operation by the insulated-outside-rail method.

thing. A line of flexible track, manufactured and distributed for many years by the GarGraves Trackage Corporation, features more prototypical T-shaped rails and is available with the middle rail blackened to help hide it from the eye (fig. 1-1).

GarGraves track can be bent to curves of any diameter, allowing layout designers to avoid the mathematical symmetry of fixed-diameter sectional track. However, the need for shaping it by hand and cutting it to size has discouraged many modelers from using it. You can easily master these skills, though they do require more time than does assembling sectional track.

Another advantage of GarGraves track over Lionel concerns the rails. Because they're mounted on wooden ties, all three are naturally insulated from one another. On Lionel-type sectional track, however, the two outer rails are electrically connected through the metal ties. To operate accessories through the insulated-outside-rail method, you have to buy or make special sections of Lionel-type track. With GarGraves track, making an insulated outside rail requires only inserting a fiber or plastic track pin in each end.

More recently, several manufacturers have introduced rigid sectional track that looks like the flexible kind. These products represent an excellent compromise because they look more realistic than track with metal ties but don't require bending and cutting, so they take less time to set up. They offer greatly improved appearance and more design options, thanks to the wide variety of diameters available in the curved sections. Producers make turnouts to match most of these curves. These products are described in more detail in Chapter 2.

Even so, I've designed all the plans in this book to use traditional sectional track, and most of them rely on only the diameters available from Lionel. Modelers may choose to adapt the plans by using flexible track or the new sectional products. This will result in certain improvements, such as more closely spaced double-track main lines and more space-efficient sidings. The photos in this book depict such adaptations of some of the sectional track plans.

As a common denominator, I used Lionel's O27 track, as it has the smallest circle diameter (27 inches) consistent with good operation. Lionel makes sectional track with 42"-diameter curves (O42) that matches its O27 line in appearance. Some of the plans combine these two types, although you may substitute O27 curves for those indicated as O42. Almost all the turnouts shown are either O27 or O42 in size. The uncoupling ramps specified in the drawings are the postwar (1945–69) 6019 model intended for operating

cars and both magnetic and electromagnetic knuckle couplers. A modern-era (1970–97) equivalent exists; it's item 6-12746.

Most Lionel trains will run on O27 track—even the big F3 diesels and most steam engines—although larger items look unrealistic on such sharp curves. Chapter 1 discusses how to choose equipment that looks best on O27 layouts. If you wish to run the biggest Lionel locomotives, such as the recent Mohawk and Northern steamers or the classic Fairbanks-Morse Train Master diesel, you should plan to use wider curves. Fortunately, adapting these sharp-curve plans to track with wider diameters is easy. You can build any of my designs with O gauge track (approximately 30 inches in diameter) with only a small increase in overall size. Moving up to larger diameter loops, such as Lionel's O42, O54 (54 inches), or O72 (72 inches), or the in-between curves offered by other manufacturers, allows you to use Lionel's larger locomotives and longer cars. It also improves the appearance of the trains when running.

Some of the plans include suggestions for using Lionel accessories. Because the company made so many different and fascinating items, you should feel free to make substitutions in any of the layouts, replacing a log loader with a barrel loader, for example. The only major consideration is one of space; be sure that the accessory you plan to substitute will fit.

## WIRING DIAGRAMS

Many of the track plans feature basic wiring requirements, including accessory connections and train operation by traditional *block control*, which is the most common standard for toy train wiring. These concepts have been used with Lionel trains for generations; they're reliable, relatively easy to understand, and fairly inexpensive. They also take advantage of the enormous number of powerful and reliable Lionel transformers produced during the postwar period.

The plans apply the principle of common ground with multiple transformers and use insulated outside rails for automatic accessories. I briefly describe these basic wiring techniques for Lionel trains later in this introduction, but have assumed that readers have some familiarity with them. Those of you who lack such knowledge altogether should consult the instruction books listed in Chapter 8.

The block wiring system is compatible with and easily converted to use with both walkaround throttles (including those manufactured by Dallee Electronics and All-Trol Products) and the new command control systems. Recent developments in electronics have caused a revolution in toy train control devices. Lionel's new radio-controlled TrainMaster throttle offers great flexibility and precision in multiple-train operation. Solid-state devices also have greatly improved the operation of automatic accessories, such as crossing gates and signals. Operators who possess the requisite knowledge can adopt any of these concepts to the track plans in this book. Using Lionel's Train-Master system eliminates the need for isolated electrical blocks, for example. In addition, you can substitute optical or current flow sensors for insulated outside rails. (Texts with information about these products are listed in Chapter 8.)

For convenience, I refer to just two Lionel transformers: the common 1033, a 90-watt model that came with most O27 sets during the postwar period, and the powerful, 275-watt ZW. Lionel made many other transformers in a variety of sizes, and except for the smaller ones, any may be used for the applications described in this book. In Chapter 3, a chart of the various transformers shows which connections should be used for throttles and fixed-voltage applications.

In brief, the following seven parameters apply to the track plans described in this book:
- Sectional track, O27 and O42 curves
- O27 turnouts, postwar 1122 or modern-era 5121 and 5122, and O42 turnouts
- Uncoupling ramps, postwar 6019 or modern-era 6-12746
- 1033 and ZW transformers
- Block control wiring
- Common ground
- Insulated-outside-rail accessory control

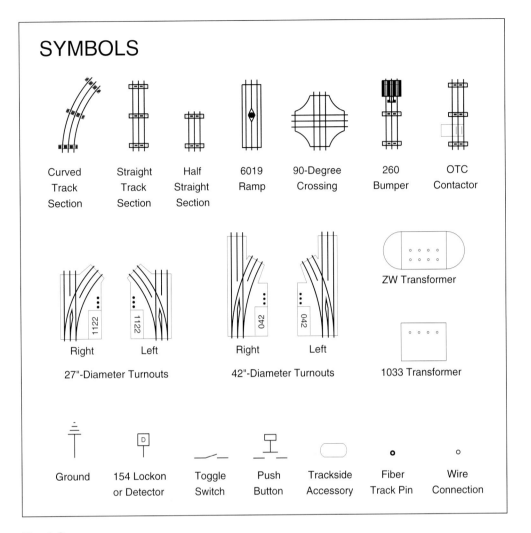

**SYMBOLS**

Curved Track Section / Straight Track Section / Half Straight Section / 6019 Ramp / 90-Degree Crossing / 260 Bumper / OTC Contactor

27"-Diameter Turnouts — 1122 Right, 1122 Left / 42"-Diameter Turnouts — 042 Right, 042 Left / ZW Transformer / 1033 Transformer

Ground / 154 Lockon or Detector / Toggle Switch / Push Button / Trackside Accessory / Fiber Track Pin / Wire Connection

**Fig. 1-2**

The symbols used in the plans are shown in the accompanying illustrations. The fully detailed examples are used for the principal layout or layouts in each chapter; the simplified symbols are used for alternate track plans (figs. 1-2 and 1-3).

Once you're familiar with the basic wiring conventions, tracing the connections on the diagrams is easy. I specify two transformers, a 1033 and a ZW, for all but the smallest layouts (see Chapter 3 for suitable substitutes). These two units are grounded together, and must be *in phase*. A wire connects the ground post of the 1033 (A) with the ground post of the ZW (U). Note that Lionel wasn't consistent in the labeling of transformer posts. The chart in Chapter 3 identifies ground posts on all common transformers.

To check whether the two transformers are in phase, connect their ground posts together and attach a wire to a throttle post of the ZW, either A or D. Plug in the two transformers, set their throttles at the approximate midpoint, and briefly touch the other end of the ZW throttle wire to the throttle post (U) of the 1033. If there is a strong spark, remove only the 1033 wall plug from its socket and rotate it 180 degrees and then plug it in again. When you touch the ZW post wire to the throttle post (U) of the 1033 this time, there should be little or no spark, indicating that the transformers are in phase. Put a dot of white paint on the left side of *both* transformer wall plugs, so you'll always find it easy to plug them in properly. **CAUTION: Never operate two interconnected transformers without ensuring that they are in phase.** Once you determine the proper phasing, it is best to plug them both permanently into a power bar.

For simplicity, I've indicated the ground connection to the layout by a triangular symbol as shown. Wherever this symbol appears, you can assume that a wire connects all of these points. (When building a layout, be sure to run a ground wire in a big loop around the perimeter or to any location where there are numerous tracks or accessories. This allows easy connection of everything to the ground circuit.) Note that only *one* of the outside running rails of the track is shown connected

to a ground symbol. With sectional track, *both* running rails will be grounded through the metal ties, except for sections with one insulated outside rail. If you use lock-ons, clip 2 is the ground connection.

The ZW transformer has two throttles, labeled A and D; either may be used, and on large layouts, *both* may be used by connecting them to different parts of the main line. The throttle post connects to the *middle* rail of the track (clip 1 on a lockon). The way in which the throttle is connected provides a system of *block control*.

Figure 1-4 shows three simple blocks of track, separated from each other by fiber or plastic track pins in the middle rail. One such pin is shown between the second track section from the right and the 6019 uncoupling ramp section next to it. The other fiber pin separates the section at the far left from the section to its right.

One wire from throttle D is connected to one terminal on each of three single-pole single-throw (SPST) toggle switches. The other terminal of the right-hand toggle is wired to the middle rail of the right-hand block of track. Closing this toggle sends power from the throttle to the middle rail of that block, but not to the others, as the fiber pin in the middle rail stops the flow of current.

The other two toggles are wired to the other two blocks as shown. Operators now have the option of turning any of the three blocks on or off. A train will run in any "on" block and will stop in any "off" block. On an actual layout, therefore, you could turn off a train on a siding while running another train on the main line.

Wherever a wire connects to the track or another wire, the connection is shown by a small circle. Wires that are shown crossing each other or track sections are assumed not to be

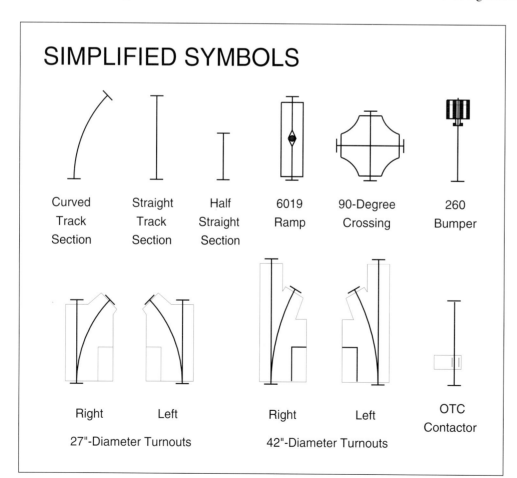

## SIMPLIFIED SYMBOLS

| Curved Track Section | Straight Track Section | Half Straight Section | 6019 Ramp | 90-Degree Crossing | 260 Bumper |

| Right | Left | Right | Left | OTC Contactor |
| 27"-Diameter Turnouts | | 42"-Diameter Turnouts | |

**Fig. 1-3**

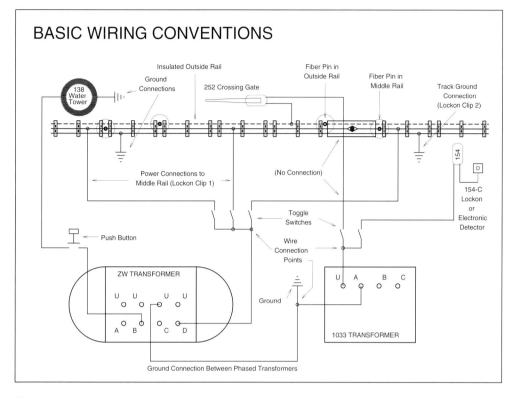

**BASIC WIRING CONVENTIONS**

Fig. 1-4

connected if this circle is missing. (Wires terminating in accessories are not marked with circles.)

## ACCESSORY ACTIVATORS

Beginning in the middle 1930s, Lionel made special switches called *contactors,* pressure-operated devices placed under the ties of the track. The weight of a passing train closes these switches to operate such accessories as crossing gates. The track must be free to move up and down for these switches to work properly. On permanent layouts, where the track is securely mounted to a table, an alternate system is needed. To fill this need, Lionel and K-Line Electric Trains sell straight track sections with one outer rail insulated from the metal ties by fiber strips.

You can also make an insulated track section yourself. Just pry up the metal tie fingers that hold the rail in place, cut small rectangles of thin automotive gasket material to fit over the rail so that it looks like the middle rail, and put it back together. Bend the tie fingers down securely, though not hard enough to puncture the gasket material. Then put a plastic or fiber track pin in each end of the rail. (Several of the books in Chapter 8 show this process in detail.)

Now you can connect automatic accessories to these insulated outside running rails; such rails are shown in

the diagrams as dashed lines instead of solid ones. Simple action accessories, such as the 252 crossing gate at top center, require only two connections. One wire must be attached to a power source, in this case the variable-voltage throttle post of the 1033 transformer. The other connects to the insulated rail.

The 1033 transformer has two possible fixed-voltage posts available when the A post is used as a ground. The B post would provide 5 volts, but this isn't enough to operate a 252 crossing gate. The C post provides 16 volts, which would make the gate go down very fast. Instead, use the throttle post (U), which allows an operator to adjust the amount of voltage flowing to the gate, thereby precisely regulating the speed at which it will descend.

You may also use one of the accessory posts of the ZW to run such automatic accessories. These posts (B and C) can also be adjusted to any voltage between 6 and 20. However, there is one significant advantage of using a separate transformer. If the ZW is used to run both the trains and the operating accessory, the gate will draw off some power from the circuit when it goes down and cause the train to slow down slightly. (With smaller transformers, or if several accessories are activated at one time, the train may slow down significantly.) Using an independent transformer keeps the flow of current to the train constant.

Note that a toggle switch is provided in the power wire from the U post of the 1033 to the gate. This allows you to turn it off. (For example, you may have a train sitting for a long time in front of the gate and want to keep the gate from overheating.) The other wire from the accessory is connected to the insulated outside rail as shown. You may use clip 2 of a lockon at this location, but be sure to mount the lockon on the same side as the insulated rail.

In the diagrams, the limits of each insulated running

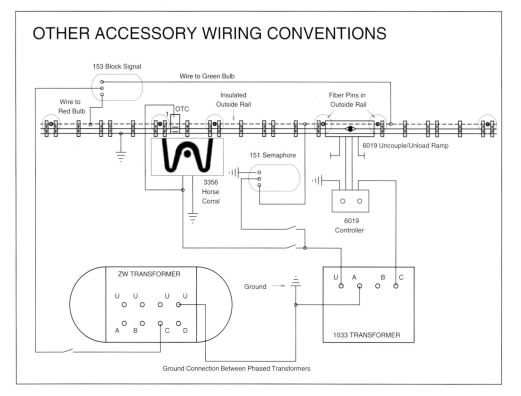

**Fig. 1-5**

ered by the U post of the 1033 transformer. The 154 has three binding posts for connection of wires, one for each bulb and one common. The common post is the one that isn't separated from the base of the signal by an insulating washer. Connect the transformer power wire to this common post. If you use Lionel's special 154-C track lockon, connect the other two wires to clips 2 and 3; do not use clip 1. (This lockon is not shown mounted on the track in the diagrams, but is, instead, symbolized by a square enclosing the letter D, for detector.)

rail are shown as circles, representing the plastic or fiber track pins. Note that in the example, there are *three* sections of track with insulated outer rails connected together and that fiber pins are necessary only at the outer ends of the three-section grouping. Because of these fiber pins, the insulated rail is not connected to the ground circuit. Even though power is going from the transformer to the gate, without a ground connection to complete the circuit, the current cannot flow, and the gate does not operate.

When a train enters the insulated section, its metal wheels touch *both* of the outside running rails, the insulated one and the *grounded* one on the opposite side. The ground connection passes through the wheels and axles from the grounded rail to the insulated one and then to the gate, completing the circuit and causing the gate to go down. The gate will stay down as long as there is a train on the insulated section.

Among the other Lionel accessories you can wire in this manner are the 45N automatic gateman (not the model 145; see below), the 140 banjo signal, 125 whistling station, 128 animated newsstand, 155 ringing signal, and 262 crossing gate. Any automatic accessory that has a constantly burning light, however, will be wired differently, as described later in this section.

I've shown yet another accessory, the 154 highway warning flasher (the familiar crossbuck signal), pow-

You also have the option of wiring any of these accessories through electronic detectors, which are sold by the manufacturers listed in Chapter 8. Most of these detectors, except for the optical ones, are used in conjunction with an insulated outer rail. Using detectors offers certain advantages, such as greater independence in power supply and consumption, and a more even flashing rate for 154 signals than a track lockon provides. Further details may be obtained from the texts listed in Chapter 8.

Simple voluntary accessories (those intended to be activated by an operator instead of a passing train) are commonly connected to the main transformer. Since they're most often used when trains are stopped, such as a water tower when a locomotive is taking on water, you need not worry whether the extra power drain causes a train to slow down.

The 138 water tower, for example, has only two binding posts. One is wired to the ground circuit and the other to post B of the ZW transformer through a normally-off push button. Post B is adjusted to a voltage level (probably 12 to 14) that will allow the spout to descend in a slow, realistic fashion. The tower operates only when someone pushes its button.

Other common Lionel accessories have slightly different wiring patterns (fig. 1-5). No special attention is needed for the 1122-style turnout, which operates from track power. Just connect the three wires from the controller to the three binding posts of the turnout. (More sophisticated options are available, however; see the second volume of *Wiring Your Lionel Layout* and *Tips and Tricks for Toy Train Operators* in Chapter 8.) The 6019 uncouple/unload ramp also can be used just as it comes from the box, with four wires leading to its control panel. But using the ramp in this way requires power in the track at all times, which isn't always possible (for example, when you're using locomotives that lack a neutral position between forward and reverse).

## UNCOUPLE/UNLOAD RAMPS AND OTC CONTACTORS

You can provide the 6019 with fixed voltage from the transformer, independent of track power, by disconnecting the right-hand wire at the ramp and connecting it to post C of a 1033 transformer. This gives it a constant 16 volts, enough for snappy uncoupling action and plenty of power for operating milk cars and cattle cars. (If the milkman throws the cans too violently, use post B or C of the ZW instead, and adjust it to a voltage that gives the best performance.)

The other three wires may be left intact. Alternatively, you can disconnect the left-hand wire and attach it directly to the ground circuit. This is advisable when the uncouple/unload ramp is located far from the control panel. (This wiring pattern works for all 1019, 6019, and RCS ramps. If you use the O gauge UCS-type or its modern successor, the 5530, attach the second wire from the right to the fixed-voltage post and not the right-hand wire.) For clarity, uncouple/unload ramp connections aren't shown on any of the layout plans.

Some operating cars specify an OTC contactor instead of a 6019 type. These include such items as the 3356 horse car and corral and the 3562 barrel car. The power wire runs through a toggle switch (or push button, if you don't mind holding it down while the car and corral operate) to one of the clips on the corral and to clip 1 of the OTC lockon; do not use clip 2. When connected in this fashion, the corral operates whenever you turn on the toggle, even if the horse car isn't present, so the horses can be allowed to mill around inside the fence. When a car is in place in front of the corral, its doors will open and the horses can enter and exit.

Placement of the OTC contactor is critical; it must be directly below one of the car's trucks when the doors are lined up with the corral chutes. You may also use a 6019 ramp instead of an OTC contactor, though this would cause the car to be independent of the corral circuit and would require you to push the *uncouple* button

to make it work. **CAUTION: Using the unload button will short-circuit the car.** Power for this installation can come from the U post of the 1033 or one of the adjustable posts (B or C) of the ZW. Because the horse car is sensitive to voltage level and the horses are likely to fall over if given too much power, you'll find an adjustable voltage post is preferable to a fixed voltage post such as C on the 1033.

Some automatic trackside accessories with action circuits are intended to be illuminated when not operating. These include the 145 automatic gateman, 151 semaphore, and 445 operating switch tower. All have three binding posts, or clips: one for the bulb, one for the action device, and one that is common to both. You should connect the fixed-voltage wire to the common post (the middle one on the 151 semaphore, for example) through a toggle switch, so you can turn it off when necessary. The bulb post connects to the ground circuit, and the action post connects to an insulated outside rail.

When wired this way, the semaphore will be illuminated whenever the toggle switch is turned on; the semaphore's arm will operate only when a train reaches the insulated outer rail. A 145 gateman or 445 switch tower will work the same way, remaining illuminated at all times yet operating only in the presence of a train.

## BLOCK SIGNALS

The 153 block signal and related items (148 dwarf signal, 450 signal bridge, and similar items) have red and green bulbs that can be wired to light alternately according to the position of a train. Using Lionel's 153C under-the-track contactor, one of the bulbs is always illuminated, though this isn't prototypical. A more realistic system has the green bulb illuminated when a train approaches, then turns the signal to red when the train passes by to warn other following trains.

There are three binding posts to be connected—one for the green bulb, one for the red, and one common to both. Voltage from the ZW transformer post C connects to the common post through a toggle switch. The green bulb wire connects to an insulated running rail located so that the green bulb will illuminate when the train is approaching. The red bulb is connected to another insulated rail on the other side of the signal, so that it will illuminate when the train has passed. These two insulated rails should be positioned about one average train length apart so the bulbs will illuminate alternately and not at the same time.

With some of the plans in this book, I provided specific wiring diagrams for accessories in order to suggest suitable locations for the insulated outside running rails. You can alter these locations to suit your needs or wishes. In fact, you can modify any of the plans by substituting other accessories or relocating the ones I've specified. I encourage experimentation of this nature so that you can personalize a layout.

Every layout benefits from nonoperating illuminated accessories, such as lamp posts, stations, floodlight towers, and various kinds of houses, stores, and businesses. I've omitted these from the plans, though you'll notice them in many of the photos. Wiring these accessories is simple: each bulb has one connection to the ground circuit and one to an appropriate voltage post, such as B or C on the ZW. The 1033 transformer has an ideal fixed-voltage circuit that provides 11 volts, just right for a good level of illumination. Unfortunately, this circuit involves posts B and C, and can't be used with the common ground. However, you can easily run a separate ground loop from post B to all of these lighted accessories, along with a power wire from C through a toggle switch, so you can turn them off. Just make certain that there's no connection between the common ground (post A) and the lighting circuit ground (B).

## TABLE CONSTRUCTION

There are many different methods of table construction suitable for toy train layouts, from flat surfaces made out of 4 x 8-foot sheets of plywood to the L-girder style favored by scale modelers. The latter method allows for infinitely variable grades and levels of track and such scenic effects as hills, valleys, and waterways. Consult any of the many instruction books that are available, a number of which are listed in Chapter 8 for those who wish to explore these techniques.

In a search for speed and simplicity, I have built most of my layouts on hollow-core doors, which are available from building supply firms in a standard 6'8" length and a variety of widths. These doors are self-supporting and require no framework other than legs to place them at the desired height. They also are relatively economical and nicely finished, and can easily be cut to form rivers and lakes. Their major disadvantage is noise, since they're hollow and so amplify the sound of the trains. Using cork roadbed minimizes this annoyance, however. All the plans are of modular design, using one or more of these doors. Chapter 7 describes construction techniques.

Now we proceed to designing our toy train layout. Before deciding on a ready-made track plan or creating an original one, a prospective operator should address a number of questions to identify and define an overall concept for the design. We explore these questions in Chapter 2.

# 2

# DEFINING THE CONCEPT

Beginning with the early childhood Lionel pikes that wandered around and beneath the furniture on my bedroom floor, I have designed and built many dozens of layouts in Standard, O, HO, and N scales and currently have seven different layouts in operation. One is in my office at Acadia University, another is in my wife's office there, and my wife's mother has donated her basement to the cause of our standard gauge pike. At home we have four more, one of them a portable unit that can be transported to schools, train meets, and other suitable locations. On average, I dismantle and rebuild one layout each year.

The success of these efforts has varied considerably. Some layouts have kept me endlessly fascinated, while others bored me before I'd driven the last spike. The factors that determine my continued interest in a layout are directly related to those aspects of operation that I enjoy most. And what *I* enjoy may not be what another modeler is most interested in. Therefore, novice layout planners should first ask themselves a series of questions that will assist in shaping the concept. Use *your own answers* to guide you in selecting a plan from the chapters that follow.

## QUESTION 1: WHAT TYPE OF OPERATION DO YOU ENJOY MOST?

Some people just like to watch the trains run. (I class myself in this category much of the time.) For this type of modeler, a layout should include continuous loops, as many as the available space will allow without crowding. A double- or triple-track main line with crack passenger trains overtaking laboring freights offers great visual satisfaction, with a minimum of operator intervention.

Other modelers love switching operations. (My

Fig. 2-1. Operating from the catenary wires, a Lionel GG1 passes by a variety of locomotives on parallel sidings in the yard area of the author's largest layout.

Fig. 2-2. Short locomotives and cars from the 1920s and '30s make it possible to run passenger trains on compact O gauge layouts. The author's Red Comet set on the upper track has coaches measuring only 7½ inches long.

most frequent visiting engineer, Bob Rushton, falls into this category.) If coupling and uncoupling, making up trains, and using a variety of motive units are your greatest pleasures, plan on including a marshaling yard or a number of storage sidings, along with towns and industries to give your trains logical destinations.

Maybe you like lots of action. With their small-diameter trackage and plenty of switches, Lionel trains make it possible to put all the activity of a Class One railroad into a modest-sized pike. Plan on more track than scenery, and install a variety of operating accessories to keep you interested. (If you want to see just how much railroad activity can be packed onto a single 4 x 8-foot sheet of plywood, consult Roland LaVoie's book, *Model Railroading with Lionel Trains,* listed in Chapter 8. His track plan crams an unbelievable amount of action into a relatively small space.)

If you are fascinated with gadgets, plan on including all the wonderful operating cars and trackside accessories that Lionel has produced over the years. Your layout will need lots of remote-control track sections and sufficient space between the tracks to accommodate coal elevators, newsstands, lift bridges, rotating beacons, and radar towers, as well as freight handlers that load everything from logs to barrels to culverts to scrap metal.

Perhaps you like the satisfaction of creating your own world in miniature, with all the fine details of the real thing. In that case, you'll probably find a single-track main line surrounded by lots of open space for buildings and scenery most satisfying. Such enthusiasts view their trains less as the main focus of the layout and more as an integral part of a true representation of a community. If space permits (a long hallway, for example, or a full-length attic or basement), you may want a point-to-point pike, with a town at each end, although such designs are beyond the scope of this book. Whatever your design, remember that in the *real* world, trains don't run round and round; they *go* somewhere.

Another area of interest is the accumulation of a large variety of motive power. If your goal is to acquire an example of every possible type of steam or diesel locomotive, plan on assembling a yard area with plenty of storage sidings. You'll need a turntable or a diesel transfer table to use the space efficiently, because regular turnouts take up a lot of room when used for sidings. On my largest layout, a transfer table serves 22 sidings to create a busy yard area adjacent to the main line (fig. 2-1).

## QUESTION 2: WHAT KIND OF TRAINS DO YOU LIKE TO RUN?

The type of trains you most enjoy can significantly influence the kind of layout you build and the way you arrange the trackage. Passenger trains are beautiful to watch, with their long, sinuous shape and brightly lighted windows. They look best on a layout with depots, platforms, parking areas for cars so people can meet the trains, and roads that lead into town.

Freight trains are interesting and colorful, with the many shapes of box, tank, hopper, stock and other revenue-producing cars. They need freight stations and industries to make use of their cargo-carrying purpose, along with lots of sidings to park those boxcars and gondolas beside the loading docks.

Work trains are rugged and businesslike. With their cranes and searchlight cars, bunk and tool cars, and such things as snowplows and water tankers, they need a reason for existing. They look best when stored in a yard area or in a section of the layout where a crew is laying new rails.

## QUESTION 3: HOW MUCH SPACE CAN YOU DEVOTE TO THE LAYOUT, AND WHAT SHAPE IS THE AVAILABLE AREA?

Unless you live in a closet, you have enough room for a Lionel layout. The one shown in Chapter 3 occupies a space just 30 inches on each side. Other options are possible, even in small houses or apartments, such as the coffee-table railroad shown in Chapter 4. If you have a train room, but if it must be used for other purposes on a regular basis, consider a high-level, around-the-room pike that's mounted on shelves along the walls and above the tops of the highest furniture. If the shelves are narrow, they will protrude very little into living areas. You won't have much space for buildings or scenery, but a fairly long main line will be possible. In addition, you should plan for removable bridges at doorway locations.

With a layout of this nature, you can even run the trains close to the ceiling and above the level of windows and door frames. Watching the trains from below is unusual, and scenery on such a pike is superfluous, but running the trains turns out to be great fun. Many hobby shops have similar installations for display purposes; sometimes the builders mount them on Plexiglas roadbed for even greater visibility.

If the only available space is a spare room or a corner of a bedroom or den, two basic styles of layout are possible. If you like long trains, locate the layout around the walls. If you prefer operating accessories, a compact city area, or lots of switching, put an island layout in the center of the room. From any location, you can see the whole thing at once and keep an eye on all the action. Each of the designs in this book is an island-type layout. (Larger areas, of course, increase your options. A good-sized basement or attic is the most satisfactory location

Fig. 2-3. In addition to its well-known line of flexible track (right), the Gar-Graves Trackage Corporation has introduced sectional curves, with the rails rigidly mounted on closely spaced plastic ties. Similar products are available from Ross Custom Switches, among other manufacturers (see Chapter 8). These two examples, in 72" diameter (second from the left) and 42" diameter (third from the left), look more realistic than the typical sectional toy train track (left).

for point-to-point pikes or around-the-room layouts with wide-radius curves.)

Depending on your answers to the first two questions, you may discover that you have to make a few compromises regarding your layout. For example, if the space available is severely limited, but you really want to run a passenger service, consider collecting equipment made before the Second World War. Lionel made a variety of colorful tinplate coaches, some barely 5¹/₂" long. They have a particular charm, especially when they're combined with accessories and buildings from the same period (fig. 2-2). Decide what is most important to you, and look for a solution that will satisfy your desires; that's part of the fun of this hobby.

## QUESTION 4: HOW DO YOU WANT YOUR LAYOUT TO LOOK?

Is a realistic appearance important to you? If so, you should think about using flexible track or the new sectional pieces with plastic ties (fig. 2-3). If you have room, consider wide-radius curves, as trains look much better on them than on conventional O27 curves. Although somewhat more expensive than ordinary sectional track, the newer products with closely spaced ties are much less toylike and are quicker to install than the flexible variety. Many different diameter curves are available, making double-track main lines and closely spaced sidings easy to achieve.

As explained in Chapter 1, I designed all the plans in

this book to use Lionel turnouts with either 27"- or 42"-diameter curves. This allows the layouts to be built compactly, but there is nothing to prevent a modeler from using broader curves and more gradual turnouts if space permits. Turnouts are made in a wide variety of configurations, including three-way designs, wyes, and even curved turnouts providing two different diameters. Suppliers are listed in Chapter 8.

Obviously, realism is not compatible with cramming track into every available square inch. The world just doesn't look like that. You'll want to leave room for houses, lawns, roads, maybe a business district (fig. 2-4), and perhaps some open countryside or a small wooded area. Should your taste run toward urban areas, plan on leaving enough space for city blocks, streets, and maybe an expressway.

If operating trains takes precedence over appearance in your view, or if you don't enjoy building scenery, plan for lots of trackage. This concept is also compatible with showcasing a large number of operating accessories. Sharp curves with numerous turnouts and sidings may not be strictly true to life, but they make for plenty of action and operating excitement. If you have children in the house, they will probably appreciate this kind of layout best.

## QUESTION 5: DO YOU LIKE TO OPERATE, OR ARE YOU A HANDS-OFF WATCHER?

The answer to this question will govern how you plan the wiring for your layout. If you enjoy keeping

Fig. 2-4. This Lionel City station on the author's layout receives long streamliners and heavyweight coaches pulled by massive steam locomotives. The passenger trains enter the station gracefully on O72 curves.

several trains running at one time, avoiding collisions at crossings and making frequent stops at stations and industries, you'll need either a sophisticated block system or a command control throttle like the new Lionel TrainMaster. In that case, you must carefully plan where to locate insulated track pins for blocks and accessory control rails. Figure them out before you install the track.

If your main pleasure comes from watching just one or two trains run unassisted, you may not need a complex wiring pattern. A direct connection between the throttle and the main line should be adequate. Just be sure before you build. Dividing a layout into insulated blocks after you've laid the track and installed the scenery can be a lot of work.

## QUESTION 6: WHAT KIND OF LOCOMOTIVES AND ROLLING STOCK DO YOU PREFER?

Lionel's Reading Lines and Chessie System T-1 steam locomotives are massive, powerful, and impressive, and neither will go around an O27 gauge loop. In fact, even though they can negotiate an O42 circle, they look best on O72 curves, as fig. 2-5 shows. If you must have these monsters but have limited space at present, your choices are plain: move or add on to the family homestead! A big locomotive squeezed into a small layout is neither practical nor satisfying. It just looks silly.

The same is true of large passenger cars, such as the aluminum sets made by Lionel since the early 1950s or the heavyweight Madison cars that first appeared before the Second World War. These cars may be shorter than scale length; nevertheless, their large proportions are unsuited to really sharp curves. Williams and Weaver make similar cars in full scale lengths, which means they need even more room to look good.

Locomotives and rolling stock can help to create an illusion of size. All Lionel trains are not built to the same scale proportions. The big Standard O cars introduced in recent years are massive and close to scale. Consequently, they make a small layout seem even smaller. By contrast, the little O27 boxcars and tank cars

Fig. 2-5. The Chessie Steam Special T-1 locomotive needs broad curves and open countryside to look right, as shown on the O72 main line on the author's layout.

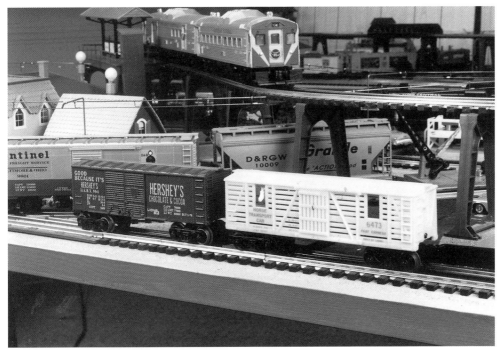

Fig. 2-6. Rolling stock intended for O27 train sets, such as the Hershey boxcar and the horse transport car shown here, can make a small layout seem less crowded. The Standard O cars in the background need much more room.

(fig. 2-6) that were introduced after the Second World War and are still made in many different road names and color schemes help preserve the image of adequate space, even when rounding the sharpest curves.

Small passenger cars are available, too. Beginning with the 2400 series, Lionel offered plastic cars that were smaller in all proportions—length, width, and height—and look fine when pulled by small locomotives around sharp curves. They have substantially less overhang than do the O gauge aluminum cars and require less clearance with the scenery when going around curves.

Another possible solution is the small prewar equipment, such as the 800-series freight cars and the tiny trains made during the early Depression years by Lionel's Winner subsidiary and American Flyer's

Fig. 2-7. Choose the size of your trains to suit the size of your layout. These tiny Winner trains, built by Lionel in the Depression, don't overpower even this smallest of all layouts, a loop of O27 track.

Champion line. They run on O27 track, yet are small enough to make a convincing layout possible in an area that's as small as a square yard (fig. 2-7).

## SUMMARY

If you take the time to consider carefully each of the foregoing questions, you'll acquire great insight into your own likes and dislikes and be better able to plan a layout that keeps your interest. Now let's begin our exploration of layout design with a pike that anyone can have, no matter how limited space may be. It occupies no more area than an end table and even can be hung on a wall and collapsed to a depth of less than 8 inches when not in use.

# 3

# THE MOST BASIC LAYOUT

Everyone who collects trains has enough room for a Lionel layout. If you display your trains on shelves on the wall, you can put a hideaway layout in the same amount of space.

My wife, Gay, is a seasoned collector with a special fondness for the tiny trains made between the First and Second World Wars: diminutive Lionel 150 locomotives and 800-series freight cars, Winner and Lionel Junior sets, and American Flyer Champion steam engines and rolling stock. Her layout takes up an area only 32 inches on each side, and when hung on the wall and closed, it projects just $7^1/_2$ inches into the room. Even with the drop-front layout in position for running the trains, it extends outward just a little more than 3 feet (fig. 3-1).

## OVERALL DESIGN

I built Gay's layout in a wall-mount cabinet, with interior shelves to hold part of her collection. The trains circle a single loop of original Winner Corporation track, passing a Winner transformer station, a 184 bungalow and a 93 water tower. Two Lionel operating accessories provide sound and lights: a 69 warning bell signal and an early 76 block signal. I mounted the taller items on hinges (fig. 3-2), so they fold down to allow the cabinet to close. There are roads and driveways and lawns, along with enough small details to give the layout life, all contained within a space less than 3 feet square.

Despite its tiny size and admittedly limited track design, this basic layout illustrates most of the principles involved in layout planning. Its endless loop allows continuous running, the station gives passengers and freight a destination, and the accessories respond to the passing trains with changing lights and a shrill bell to warn the traffic. Because of the layout's simplicity, it requires only a small power source (fig. 3-3).

Fig. 3-1. The author's wife, Gay, runs her tiny 60-year-old Winner and American Flyer Champion trains on this fold-up wall layout. Shelves in the cabinet display part of her collection, while the trains travel through authentic scenery straight out of an old-time Lionel catalog.

Fig. 3-2. Taller accessories (mounted on hinges) are lowered to lie flat against the layout, in preparation for folding up the platform into its wall-mounted storage box.

Gay's first acquisition in the "tiny train" category was a Winner passenger set consisting of a 1010 New Haven–type electric locomotive, two 1011 Pullman cars, a 1012 lithographed transformer station, and a 27-inch circle of track, all neatly packed in its original box. This Depression-era set forms the foundation of her layout. The beautifully decorated station (the same structure used later by Lionel for the 48W whistle station) contains a tiny transformer with just enough output to run the miniature electric motor that powers the locomotive at a moderately slow speed.

## WIRING DETAILS

Unfortunately, the transformer has no reserve capacity for lights or accessories. Adding even one illuminated building to the layout caused the train to slow down measurably, and any operating accessory drains its current completely, bringing everything to a halt. Nor could it

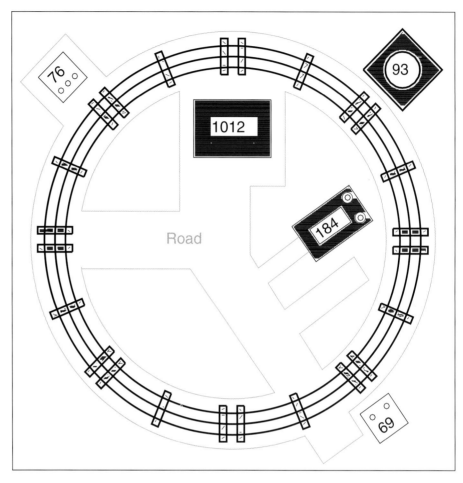

Fig. 3-3

run most of Gay's other locomotives, which contain larger motors and require more amperage. Although the station is a central focal point of the layout, it isn't functional. I chose, instead, a more powerful 1040 transformer from the late 1930s (seen at left in the background in the photo).

I wired the track as shown in fig. 3-4. There are two binding posts on the transformer, and I connected one by a wire to the middle rail (clip 1 on a Lionel lockon). I attached the wire from the second binding post, the ground wire, to the outside rails (lockon clip 2). Note that on this simple layout, only one ground wire is needed; however, the wiring diagram shows the same ground symbols that will be used in the more complex diagrams in this book. The dotted line between the symbols, indicating that they are connected, won't appear on layout diagrams in subsequent chapters, although the connection is understood.

The 184 bungalow, which is illuminated by a 12-volt bulb, is connected to the track by another lockon, one wire to the middle rail (clip 1), and one to the outer rails

(clip 2). I could have run longer wires from the bungalow to the transformer's binding posts. However, since the track is the closest source of power, the short wires leading to a track lockon seemed to me to be the most efficient way to connect the bulb.

The 69 warning bell (lower right) also requires two connections, a power source, and a ground. The power source is the middle rail, but this accessory can't be grounded to the outside running rails. Doing so would cause it to ring constantly whenever the trains are running. Instead, a section of track with an insulated running rail was provided, and I connected the ground wire from the 69 bell signal to this rail through clip 2 of a lockon located on the insulated side of the track. Whenever the metal wheels of a locomotive or car enter this section, they ground the insulated rail to the opposite running rail and cause the bell on the accessory to ring. (See Chapter 1 for an explanation of insulated rail accessory operation.)

Gay and I decided that the trains would travel clockwise on the loop. Therefore, I located the insulated rail *ahead* of the 69 signal. That way, a train starts the bell ringing before it reaches the grade crossing that this accessory protects. I positioned the signal right at the end of the insulated section, so it stops ringing just as the last car of a train passes the grade crossing.

The other operating accessory, a 76 block signal, contains a green and a red bulb. Three wires are required to connect it: one for power (the middle rail again) and one each for the two bulbs. I connected each of these two latter wires to separate insulated running rails, as shown in the diagram, so the bulbs would light alternately. The wire attached to the closest track section illuminates the green bulb as the train approaches, indicating a clear track ahead. I grounded the other wire to the same insulated section as the 69 signal. When a train reaches that point on the layout, the block signal turns red to indicate that a train is occupying the track beyond the signal.

## TWO TRANSFORMERS

At any one time, the total load on the transformer is relatively light: the locomotive motor, the bulb in the bungalow, and either the green bulb in the 76 signal or the red bulb plus the ringing bell. Nevertheless, since all items are connected to the same power source, there is some reduction in the amount of current reaching the train when either of the two accessories is operating.

This system has another drawback. The 1040 transformer has a rheostat speed control that varies the amount of voltage reaching the track, and this allows an operator to speed up or slow down the train. However, any adjustment of the speed control also affects the brightness of the bungalow and block signal lights, in addition to the strength of the bell sound. To overcome this problem, I could use a larger transformer with fixed-voltage posts.

Figure 3-5 illustrates the substitution of a 90-watt 1033 transformer, which gives the advantage of greater power output than does the 1040. More important, however, is the provision of fixed-voltage posts for accessory operation.

In Chapter 1, I described using a 1033 transformer for accessory operation in conjunction with a ZW. I placed the two transformers in phase with each other and connected their ground posts. The ZW has only one ground circuit, represented by the four interconnected U posts. On the 1033, post A was used as the ground, but this transformer offers another alternative. The B post also can serve as a ground.

With the track connected to the U post (middle rail) and the A ground post (outside running rails), a range of 5 to 16 volts is available for running the trains. This is satisfactory for postwar Lionel trains and most of those made in the modern era. However, the smaller motors in the tiny Winner and Champion locomotives run at more realistic speeds with less voltage.

If I use B and not A as the ground post, the transformer sends from 0 to 11 volts to the track, a perfect range for these tiny trains. Figure 3-5 illustrates this circuit. In addition, when post B is used as a ground, post C forms a circuit providing a constant 11 volts, which is just right for the bulbs in the 76 block signal and the 184 bungalow. The 69 warning bell signal also sounds good when operating on this amount of power.

A further refinement is the addition of toggle switches to allow an operator to turn the bungalow light and either of the accessories on or off. The power wire from fixed-voltage post C passes through toggles to one terminal on the 69 bell signal or 184 bungalow. The second wire from the bungalow light bulb is connected to the ground circuit. The second wire from the bell signal attaches to the adjacent insulated running rail. This rail is grounded by the wheels of a passing train to ring the signal.

The wire from the C post passes through a third toggle to the common wire of the 76 block signal. The red bulb wire attaches to the same insulated track section as the bell signal, and the green bulb wire connects to the closest insulated rail. Now all the accessories function as they did with the 1040 transformer, but with one important difference: the bulbs remain at a constant level of brightness no matter how fast or slow the train is moving, and the bell signal rings even if the train stops on the crossing.

One disadvantage still remains. Whenever a train activates the block signal or the bell, some current is diverted from the track and the train slows down slightly. The 1033 transformer is powerful enough to minimize this effect, which is hardly noticeable. With larger locomotives or a greater number of accessories, however, the slowing down would be much more apparent.

I can cure this problem completely by providing a second separate transformer for accessories (fig. 3-6). The transformers must be phased to each other in relation to the household current, and the two ground posts (B) have to be interconnected by a common wire (see Chapter 1 for instructions). The first transformer functions only to run the trains, with the U post connected to the middle rail and the B as the ground.

The second transformer powers the accessories. You could connect all three to the C post, providing 11 volts to each of them, but one additional refinement is

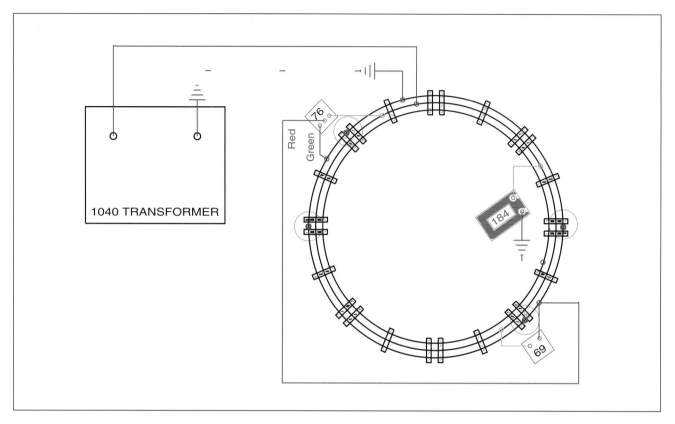

Fig. 3-4

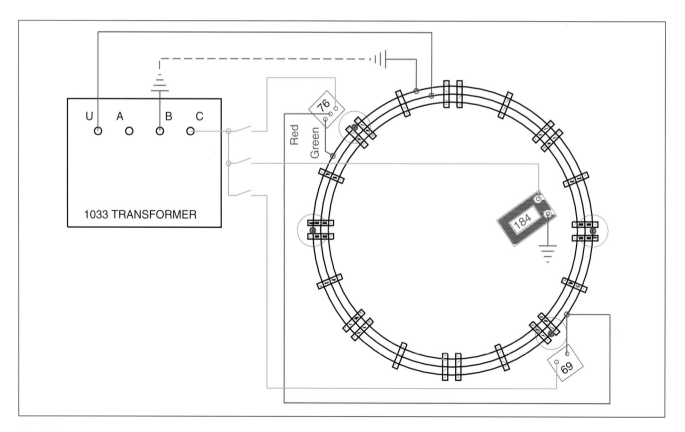

Fig. 3-5

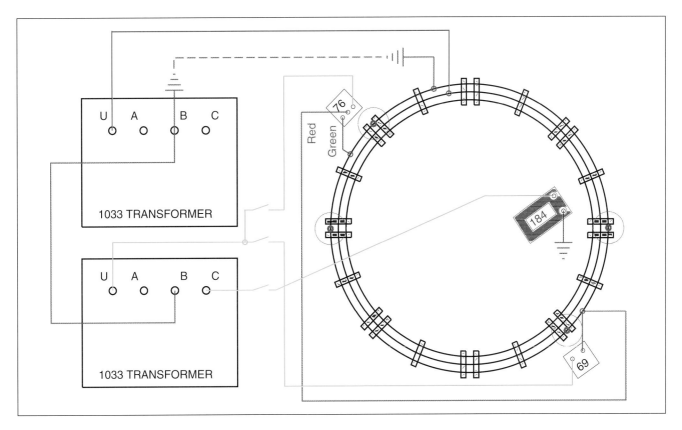

Fig. 3-6

available. While the bungalow is wired to the C post, the two operating accessories are connected to the U post. This arrangement allows an operator to adjust the amount of voltage reaching the block signal and the bell within a range of 0 to 11 volts. He or she can set the throttle at about the 9-volt level, if that's where the bell sounds best. This will cause the 76 block signal to be a bit dimmer; if you don't like this effect, connect the 76 signal to the C post as you did with the bungalow.

Having a larger transformer increases flexibility when wiring a layout, and adding a second transformer gives an operator much more precise control of all the layout's functions. You may consider using two 1033 transformers at a total of 180 watts of power to be a waste of resources for a single loop of track. If so, use two smaller transformers, perhaps 1040s or 4150s, which have been produced in great numbers by Lionel

since 1970. However, larger transformers are necessary to run trains that have more powerful motors, and plenty of reserve power is essential if you add numerous accessories.

In the chapters that follow, I'll use a 275-watt ZW transformer to run the trains and some of the accessories, while a 1033 will be shown connected to the accessories that otherwise would intermittently draw power away from the track. For smaller layouts, you can substitute any of the Lionel transformers listed in the chart below; it specifies which posts to use for variable and fixed voltages.

Although the single-loop layout described here may be perfect for very small quarters, we can have much more operating potential in little more than twice the space. I call this concept the Coffee Table Layout and describe it in Chapter 4.

| TRANSFORMER | GROUND POST | VARIABLE VOLTAGE | FIXED VOLTAGE |
|---|---|---|---|
| 1032 and 1033 | A | U (5–16 volts) | B (5 volts) C (16 volts) |
| | B | U (0–11 volts) | C (11 volts) |
| 1034 | A | U (10–20 volts) | B (6 volts) C (20 volts) |
| | B | U (4–14 volts) | A (6 volts) C (14 volts) |
| 1044 | A | U (10–20 volts) | B (6 volts) C (20 volts) |
| | B | U (6–16 volts) | C (14 volts) |
| A or Q | A | U (14–24 volts) | B (8 volts) C (14 volts) |
| | B | U (6–16 volts) | A (8 volts) C (6 volts) |
| KW | U | A (6–20 volts) B (6–20 volts) | C (6 volts) D (20 volts) |
| | C | A (0–14 volts) B (0–14 volts) | D (14 volts) U (6 volts) |
| LW | A | U (6–20 volts) | B (18 volts) C (14 volts) |
| R | A | C (14–24 volts) F (14–24 volts) | B (8 volts) D (14 volts) |
| | B | C (6–16 volts) F (6–16 volts) | A (8 volts) E (16 volts) |
| | D | none | E (10 volts) |
| RW | A | U (9–19 volts) | C (9 volts) D (19 volts) |
| | B | U (6–16 volts) | C (6 volts) D (16 volts) |
| | D | none | C (10 volts) |
| S | A | U (10–19 volts) | B (5 volts) C (19 volts) |
| | B | U (5–14 volts) | C (14 volts) |
| SW | U | A (7–18 volts) D (7–18 volts) | B (18 volts) C (14 volts) |
| TW | A | U (7–18 volts) | C (18 volts) D (14 volts) |
| | B | U (0–11 volts) | A (7 volts) |
| | E | none | F (14 volts) |
| V and Z | U | A (6–24 volts) B (6–24 volts) C (6–24 volts) D (6–24 volts) | none* none* none* none* |
| VW and ZW | U | A (6–20 volts) B (6–20 volts) C (6–20 volts) D (6–20 volts) | none* none* none* none* |

*Two of the four rheostats are set to provide fixed voltage.

# 4

# COFFEE TABLE LAYOUTS

No matter how small your house or apartment, if you have a coffee table, you can replace it with an operating Lionel layout. An entire system with a siding and even one or two reverse loops is possible in less than 18 square feet, including a station, houses, and a mountain.

The basic table is a hollow-core interior door, measuring 6'8" long and at least 30" wide. This size can accommodate a loop of O27 gauge track. With a slightly wider door (32"), you'll have more clearance between the track and the edges for scenery (fig. 4-1).

The first step is to mount a screw-on leg at each of the four corners. The length of the legs depends on how high you want the table to be above the floor (fig. 4-2). Such legs are available in a variety of lengths at hardware and building supply stores. Screw the mounting plate directly to the door close to the outer edge. Because the center area of the door is hollow, the legs must be mounted close to the sides where there is a solid framework to support them.

You can stain or paint the sides and ends of the door. Regardless of what you do, your table will look more like furniture if its edges are lined with a shaped molding, available in a variety of shapes and sizes. Thanks to the rigidity of the door, no other construction is needed, unlike more conventional model railroad tables.

As fig. 4-3 shows, a loop of track with a 180-degree curve at each end, along with five lengths of straight track on a side, takes best advantage of the available area on the table. A single left-hand turnout leads to a storage siding that's long enough to hold four cars. A remote-control uncoupling ramp next to the turnout lets you drop cars on the siding.

Fig. 4-1. The author's coffee table layout is just the right size for a small bedroom, a corner of a spare room, or a centerpiece in a living room. It is shown here in his office at Acadia University, above the computer station. The tiny pike is fully detailed and features accessories compatible with little antique trains by Lionel, Ives, and American Flyer. Note the authentic prewar 439 panel board at right, with its functional knife switches and turnout controller.

Fig. 4-2. The coffee table layout rests on four detachable legs. The hollow-core door is rigid and self-supporting, and its light weight allows it to be moved easily from place to place. Decorative molding around the edges of the door gives it a finished appearance.

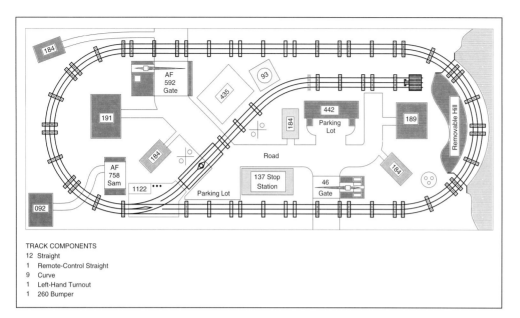

TRACK COMPONENTS
12  Straight
1   Remote-Control Straight
9   Curve
1   Left-Hand Turnout
1   260 Bumper

**Fig. 4-3**

## ACCESSORIES AND STRUCTURES

To protect one of the two grade crossings, I chose Lionel's sturdy 46 crossing gate. Along with the model 47, which has two gates flanking a double-wide roadway, this little accessory is the only gate Lionel ever made that approximates scale proportions for O27 trains.

At the back of the layout, an American Flyer 592 gate guards the second grade crossing. This accessory was also made before the Second World War, to accompany the $^3/_{16}$" scale O gauge trains that The A. C. Gilbert Company introduced in 1939 (fig. 4-4). When the American Flyer line was converted to S gauge after the war, this delicate and well-proportioned gate continued in production through 1953. Similar products have come on the market in recent years. For example, a pair of modern gates is available from Ross Custom Switches. They incorporate highway warning flashers and a ringing bell, all controlled by an electronic circuit.

Finding a diminutive substitute for Lionel's most popular accessory, the 145 gateman, proved relatively simple. Lionel introduced the gateman in 1935 for its standard and O gauge lines. The automatic action (when a train approaches, a watchman emerges from a shack swinging a lantern) is undeniably fascinating. However, the figure stands about 12 scale

feet high in O gauge, which is much too large to look right on a coffee table layout.

Once again, a similar postwar American Flyer accessory proved to be just the right size. Sam the Semaphore Man (item 758, cataloged from 1949 through 1956) features a tiny shanty with a swinging door that opens when a train arrives. As a bonus, the semaphore arm drops and its light changes from green to red (fig. 4-5).

For buildings of an appropriate size, I again turned to prewar Lionel products. The houses are from the 1920s and '30s: three 184 bungalows, a 189 villa and the impressive 191 mansion, complete with an ell that collectors usually refer to as the "train room." Although these buildings were sold for use with both standard and O gauge trains, they're actually closer to HO scale, which makes them ideal for this layout. The size discrepancy is minimized if you don't place the figures too close to the doorways, where it's obvious they would have to duck in order to enter (fig. 4-6).

For the depot, I chose a 137 station, Lionel's smallest

**Fig. 4-4. This American Flyer crossing gate, sold as part of The A. C. Gilbert Company's postwar S gauge line, is a perfect size to complement small Lionel trains.**

model with an automatic train control circuit (fig. 4-1). When wired as shown below in fig. 4-9, the station stops a train in front, delays it for ten to fifteen seconds, and then sends it on its way. Several other stations contain this feature, such as the common 132, which was made in great numbers from 1949 to 1955, and the big 115 Lionel City station. The 137 looks best with tiny trains, however.

Across the street from the station is a 442 diner (cataloged from 1938 to 1942), complete with a parking lot in front (fig. 4-7). Across the tracks is a 93 water tower, Lionel's smallest water tank. It was made in several color schemes from 1931 through 1949. Farther away and visible at the left in fig. 4-1 is an 092 illuminated signal tower (cataloged from 1923 to 1927).

The last structure of the eleven on the layout is a 435 power station (cataloged from 1926 through 1938). It stands next to the siding and appears to be sending current through the complex of power lines that stretch from pole to pole along the large street and the main line. These wires are functional; they provide electricity for the streetlights (fig. 4-8). The power station is functional, too, as it hides the transformer that powers this layout. (Lionel made three different sizes of power stations in the prewar era; the largest could hold two transformers.)

After distributing the structures about the layout, I linked them by a system of roads and sidewalks. On the right-hand side I created a hill cut from layers of foam insulation. Having a tunnel for the train to pass through helps to hide the fundamental fact that everyone on this railroad travels in circles!

## SIGNALS AND TRANSFORMERS

There are also three signals on the layout: a pair of crossbuck highways flashers and a block signal. Once again, Lionel's gigantic interpretations (models 154 and 153) would overwhelm this pike, as they're much too large to fit in with the small trains and structures. Such firms as Right-Of-Way Industries, NJ International, and Ross Custom Switches carry scale-proportioned signals that look just right on small layouts. Wiring

Fig. 4-5. Sam the Semaphore Man puts in an appearance every time a train passes by on the main line. Note the similarity in size between Sam and the O scale figure sitting on the right side of the accessory base.

Fig. 4-6. Lionel's prewar houses fit in especially well with small trains and give ample room for lawns and driveways on even the most compact of layouts.

them for insulated rail control is as easy as with the Lionel accessories.

Although I used a prewar transformer in the power station for my interpretation of the coffee table layout, you could take a more conventional approach by relying on a ZW or similar unit, as shown in fig. 4-9. The outside running rail serves as the ground and is connected to transformer post U (shown by the triangular ground symbols). There are four independent blocks, all wired through toggle switches to allow them to be turned off. The siding is one block; the main line has

Fig. 4-7. The 442 diner feeds passengers and crew during stopovers in town. The author has added eight grain-of-wheat bulbs to simulate lamps on the tables behind each window.

Fig. 4-8. The 435 power station (left) lends a typically industrial appearance to a layout, while a 93 water tower is essential for steam locomotive service.

two principal blocks, one for the left side and one for the right. I wired a two-section block to the stop station. Note the location of the fiber pins in the middle rail to separate the blocks.

Binding post 1 of the stop station receives power from the transformer, and post 2 is grounded. Connect post 3 to the middle rail of the short block as shown. The direction of travel is assumed to be clockwise. When the locomotive reaches the station, there is no power in the short insulated block, and the train coasts to a stop. The presence of the train activates the auto-

matic heat-sensitive circuit, and in 20 seconds or less the train starts again. (If you use a conventional station without this automatic feature, omit the short insulated block.)

A second transformer (1033) activates the crossing gates and Sam the Semaphore Man (fig. 4-10). Using a separate transformer prevents voltage drop at the track and allows the train to run without slowing down. The transformers are phased, and the ground posts are interconnected as shown (see Chapter 1 for details). One power wire connects to each gate and to Sam through toggle switches. The other wire from each accessory attaches to an insulated running rail.

I wired the automatic accessories to work best with trains traveling clockwise. The gates come down before a train reaches the grade crossings and go back up immediately after the last car has passed. I used several sections with insulated running rails for each accessory. Note the location of the fiber pins separating these sections; this shows the places where the approaching train starts each accessory. For example, the 46 gate is wired to four insulated sections: the straight one in front and the first three curved ones at right. As a train enters the curve at top right, the gate comes down; it goes back up immediately when the train leaves the straight section (lower right).

Sam is wired to three lengths of insulated rail directly in front of the stop station. He comes out of his shed when the train arrives and stays out until the train starts up again and travels around the left-hand curve. The American Flyer gate at the back goes down just after the train has passed Sam and goes back up as soon as the train leaves the first straight section at upper left.

The NJ International block signal has red, amber, and green bulbs. Figure 4-10 shows the insulated sections to which each is connected. As a train progresses clockwise from the top, the signal changes from green to amber to red and back to green again. Note that the insulated rail that illuminates the amber bulb also lowers the 46 gate and the rail that turns it red also triggers Sam.

Finally, the Right-Of-Way crossbuck warning signals

come with an electronic circuit board that maintains an even flash rate. I decided not to wire them to an insulated rail for automatic operation. The crossing that these signals protect goes across the siding, and if I connected them to an insulated rail on the siding, they would operate whenever a car was sitting there. Instead, I operate these signals manually, turning them on with the toggle switch on the 439 panel board (fig. 4-1) whenever I send a train onto or out of the siding.

Currently Dallee Electronics makes a circuit board (a current-sensing detector) that's ideal for automatic operation in this situation. To use it, route the power wire that goes to the middle rail of the siding through the detector, and connect the signals as shown in the instructions that come with the board. The signals will operate only when current passes through that power wire, as when a locomotive enters the siding or an illuminated car is sitting there.

These lighted signals draw much less current than do the crossing gates or the semaphore. Therefore, they're shown wired to an adjustable accessory post (B) of the ZW. This post is also used for the streetlights and the bulbs inside the

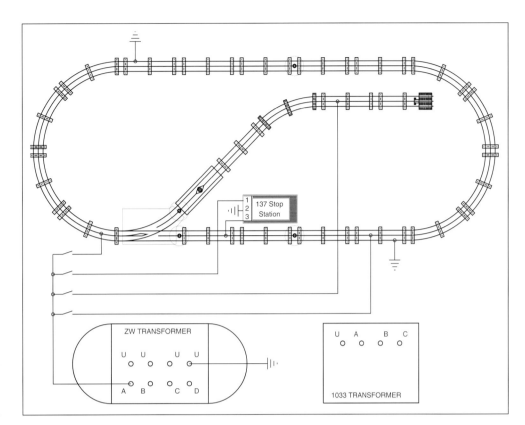

Fig. 4-9

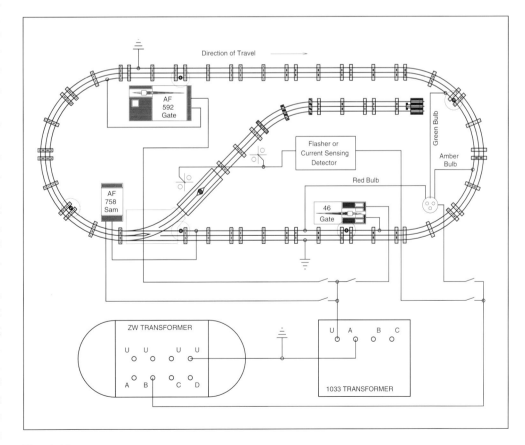

Fig. 4-10

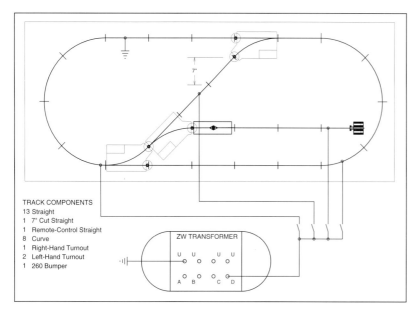

Fig. 4-11

buildings (not shown in the diagram). By setting the post to only 8 or 9 volts, you can greatly increase the life span of the bulbs. Since these lights are on constantly, there is no periodically increased drain on the transformer, and the speed of the train isn't affected.

## VARIATIONS

A minor variation on this track plan adds a pair of turnouts (one left and one right) to allow the train to reverse direction (fig. 4-11). The siding is preserved, although it's shorter. This design provides an operator with more options for train control. A train can travel counterclockwise around the loop or be diverted through either of the mainline turnouts to reverse direction and travel clockwise. To return to the original direction, the train must back up through the turnouts. Note the suggested locations for the fiber pins that separate the four blocks. If you use a stop station, add a fifth block in the same location as shown in the first layout.

You can retain all the features of the first layout, including a stop station, with this design. The main limitation is in how the crossing gates are connected. Locate the insulated sections so that the gates come down early when a train is approaching from either direction. The gates will stay down a little longer after the train has passed, but this isn't too

noticeable. If it bothers you, obtain one of the sophisticated (though expensive) detectors on the market that will control the gates properly from either direction.

The geometry of sectional track works advantageously in most situations, but for this layout to fit well within the small space available, it's best to shorten one section of straight track to about 7 inches. (This section is shown at the upper center.) You can cut Lionel track with a hacksaw; be sure that the section is held firmly in a vise during this operation. I advise placing the track between two flat boards, as the bare jaws of the vise can bend the rails. Pad the boards with fabric, and use a new fine-toothed blade and short, gentle strokes. Bearing down hard or trying to cut too quickly will distort the rails. (A Dremel Moto-Tool will make this cut quickly and easily.)

When the cut is complete, file the ends of the rails until they're smooth. The newly shortened 7" section will have only two ties. Remove the cut-off tie from the remnants of rails, and mount it on the end of the 7" section. Be sure to use the strip of fiber insulation between the tie and the middle rail.

The siding is long enough to hold three freight cars. Locate a remote-control ramp at the end as shown to allow automatic uncoupling when setting out cars. Finally, because there is more track in this design than in the previous one, there will be less room for build-

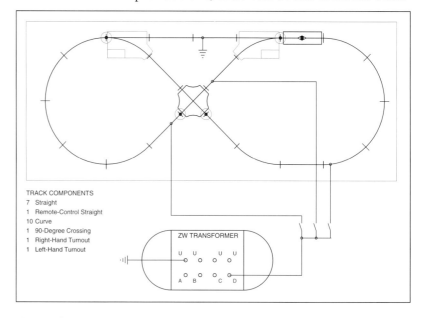

Fig. 4-12

ings and scenery. Use your imagination to create a convincing scene.

One of the most familiar track plans in the old Lionel catalogs and instruction booklets is the simple figure eight, employing a 90-degree crossing. A variation on this design is shown in fig. 4-12. If you add a pair of turnouts, your train can reverse direction an infinite number of times. I've provided suggestions for dividing this layout into three blocks, shown by the fiber pin locations and wires to the transformer in the diagram. If you want to use a stop station, I recommend locating it in front of the straight section at the lower right or in front of the remote-control ramp at the upper right. The location of other accessories and buildings is optional, according to the preferences of the builder.

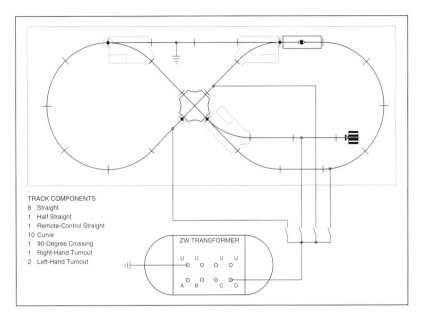

Fig. 4-13

You can even add a very short siding to this layout (fig. 4-13). Just add another left-hand turnout and a 260 bumper, mounted on a half section of straight track. The diagram doesn't show an uncoupling ramp, but you can locate one next to the turnout. However, because the siding is so short, you can uncouple only one freight car on the siding. Two cars fit if you uncouple manually.

The foregoing designs presume using a hollow-core door that's 30" or 32" wide. If you have enough room, choose a 36"-wide door instead. The extra 4 inches greatly increase the options for interesting plans. As fig. 4-14 shows, an outer loop can easily enclose three-fourths of another loop and a siding. There isn't much clearance between the track and the edges of the door, and there isn't much room left for buildings and scenery, but there are more operational possibilities.

You'll need two half sections of straight track for the outer loop shown at the extreme ends of the layout; this gives enough clearance for the inner loop. The siding is an ideal place to locate an operating accessory, such as a 397 coal loader. You can locate other freight-handling accessories along the upper or lower main lines, with other remote-control ramps installed wherever required.

If you don't need the extra running room of an interior loop, having a 36"

door will provide room for a passing siding, a stub siding for a coal unloading ramp, and extra space for buildings and scenery (fig. 4-15). Note that the very long 456 coal ramp just fits in the space available. A 362 barrel loader or a 364 lumber loader is narrow enough to go between the two tracks of the passing siding. If you prefer having more operating accessories than buildings, there is room for others inside the loop along the straight sections of the main line.

Like the other accessories, the 394 rotating beacon at the lower right is connected to post C on the main ZW transformer. With this post set at about 16 volts, all of

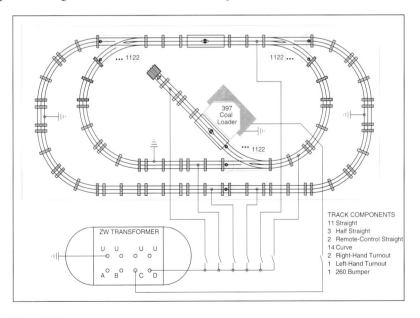

Fig. 4-14

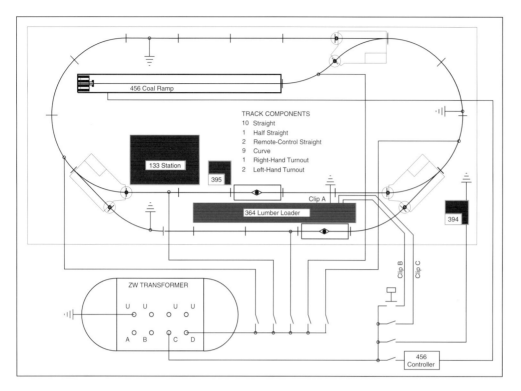

**Fig. 4-15**

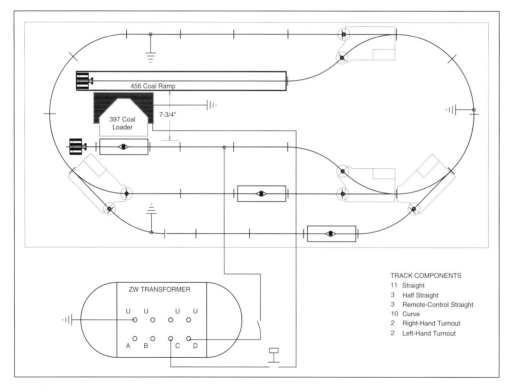

**Fig. 4-16**

to power them. If you add automatic gates, gatemen, semaphores, or banjo signals, however, wire them to a separate transformer, such as the 1033 shown in the earlier diagram (fig. 4-9). You can wire lights, such as a 395 floodlight tower and the bulb inside the 133 station, to ZW post B, set at about 9 volts for long life.

Lionel designed the 456 coal ramp to be used in conjunction with the 397 coal loader as long as it was located where coal emptied from a hopper on the ramp could drop into the loader's tray. Combining these two accessories requires a second track located 7³/₄" from the side of the loader. You can also place an uncouple/unload ramp in front of the 397 loader. This will enable you to fill it with coal from either a dump car in front or a hopper on the ramp.

Figure 4-16 adds to the previous layout the extra siding necessary for using the 397 coal loader with the 456 ramp. An extra power wire and a toggle switch are shown connected to this siding. Note the location of the right-hand fiber pin in the middle rail for the passing siding, which differs

from fig. 4-15. The 397 coal loader requires only two connections, a ground and a power wire from transformer post C through a push button or a toggle switch.

these items will work well. The beacon is on all the time, and the others are used primarily when the trains aren't running, so there's no need for a separate transformer

## UP AND AWAY

If you want interesting operation in a small place and are willing to forgo a lot of buildings or operating accessories, consider the plan in fig. 4-17. You'll need a locomotive that can climb hills easily, preferably one that is equipped with Magne-Traction. There's a loop of track in the center on the lower level (shown at the top in the diagram), divided by a backwards-S track to provide reverse loops. The train climbs a 110 trestle, beginning at the upper left, and reaches another reverse loop on the upper level. After a stop at the station, it returns to the lower level.

The bottom half of the diagram shows this upper loop as well as the visible portion of the main-level tracks. Note that the topmost two turnouts are hidden under the hill. This allows an operator to choose which tunnel the train will emerge from. Kids love the element of surprise this affords. Be sure to use nonderailing turnouts under the hill to avoid having trains jump the track if you forget to throw the proper switch.

A 110 trestle set contains 24 piers of graduated size (22 in some sets), two of each size lettered from A to L (tallest to shortest). You'll need only one of each pier from B to L, located as shown. Each pier is $1/2$" taller than the preceding one, except for L and A, which are $1/4$" different from their neighbors. This allows a more gradual transition at each end of the grade. In this plan, a slight adjustment in height is necessary.

Note that a half-section of track is used between piers A and B. With only

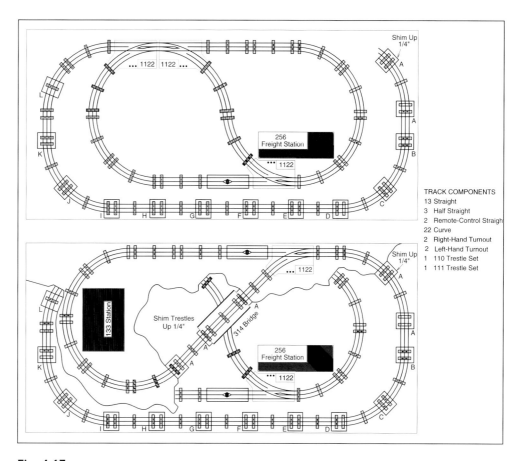

TRACK COMPONENTS
13 Straight
3 Half Straight
2 Remote-Control Straight
22 Curve
2 Right-Hand Turnout
2 Left-Hand Turnout
1 110 Trestle Set
1 111 Trestle Set

**Fig. 4-17**

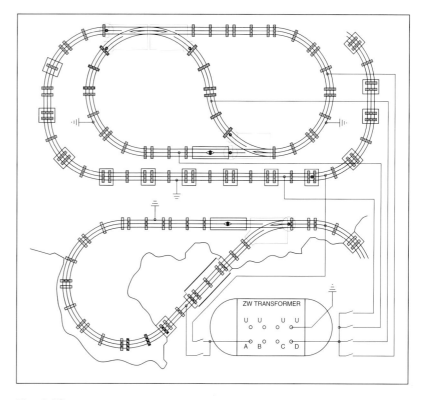

**Fig. 4-18**

## TOWN TROLLEY

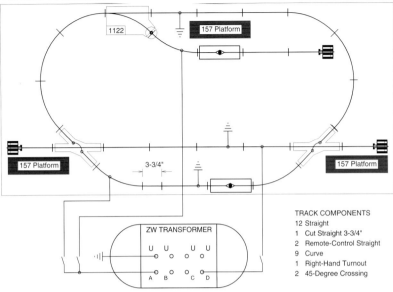

**Fig. 4-19**

have a ZW, KW, or TW with two throt-tles, you can use one for the upper loop and the upper half of the trestle and the other to control the lower half of the trestle and the main-level tracks. This allows an operator to have one train circling the lower loop while a second train maneuvers around on top of the hill. If you have an operating accessory on the upper level, using a second throttle lets you line up the train next to it without interfering with the progress of the first train around the main loop (fig. 4-18).

You can connect the wire leading from throttle A to the upper section of the trestle to the track at only one loca-tion, but be sure to use heavy-gauge wire (16- or even 14-gauge) to prevent voltage drop. The dotted line between the upper and lower halves of the dia-gram shows that the entire upper section of the trestle is powered by this wire.

## TOWN TROLLEY

The small size of a coffee table layout makes it ideal for a living room or family room, where it's available for demonstrations when guests visit. Giving such a layout a novel or entertaining operational feature increases its appeal. The Town Trolley offers just such amusement.

The basic track plan is a simple loop with a spur sid-ing. A length of straight track with bumpers at the ends

¼" difference in height between these two piers, this section maintains the same grade as the rest of the tres-tle. Install another A pier after the next section of curved track (upper right) and shim up this pier by placing a ¼" piece of plywood under its base. This pro-vides the necessary transition from grade to upper level and gives an extra ¼" clearance between the upper level and trains passing below.

In the middle of the layout, where one leg of the upper reverse loop crosses a lower track, a 314 girder bridge is used. Two A piers support this bridge, and another pier is located to its left. You must also shim each of these ¼" to place the track at the correct level.

To give the railroad plausible destina-tion points, I recommend locating one station on the upper level and another on the lower. There isn't much room for other buildings or accessories, but you could install a 397 coal loader or a 352 icing station next to the last straight sec-tion to the left of the upper loop. A plat-form for a milk car or a 3656 cattle corral would also fit in this area. A 455 oil der-rick would look good inside the lower loop behind the 256 freight station; a revolving beacon or a floodlight tower would be appropriate, too.

For this layout, you can use a trans-former with a single throttle. But if you

**Fig. 20. The central metal plate on the bottom of this Lionel crossing serves to link all the middle rails electrically.**

crosses the loop through two 45-degree crossings. This is the trolley line. The loop and siding are wired to throttle A, and the trolley line goes to throttle D.

A 60 Lionelville trolley (or one of its modern-era equivalents) on the straight track will reverse itself every time it strikes a bumper, continuing back and forth as long as current is fed to the track by the throttle. The fun comes from operating a train on the main line so as to avoid the trolley at the crossings. You can either slow down and speed up the train with throttle A or modify the speed of the trolley with throttle D. With practice, you should be able to keep both units running continuously without mishap. (A hint is in order: make your trains fairly short!)

You must modify the two crossings to achieve electrical independence of the trolley and main lines. This is indicated in fig. 4-19 by the jumper wire that connects the mainline middle rails on each crossing.

As produced, all the middle rails on these crossings were connected by an I-shaped metal plate on the underside of the crossing (fig. 4-20). To isolate the two routes, bend up the metal tabs that protrude through the plastic base, thereby releasing that part of the metal plate. Then fold over the metal plate as shown in fig. 4-21, and bend the tabs back into place against the plastic. Finally, solder a wire between the tabs from the middle rails, as shown in fig. 4-22. (Use heat sparingly so there's only enough to melt the solder. Excessive heat will melt the plastic base of the crossing.)

Although the trolley and train tracks cross each other, this concept is essentially two independent layouts on a small scale. You can eliminate the crossing by elevating one set of tracks, thus creating a type of passenger service familiar to city dwellers: an elevated line, or "el." Raising the tracks also frees valuable real estate on the main level for buildings or accessories.

## THE EL

An urban setting is the most logical concept for this layout. It consists of a conventional loop with a passing

Fig. 4-21. At the left end of the central metal plate, the tabs from the middle rail have been bent upward so the plate can be folded over. This operation is shown completed at the right end of the plate.

Fig. 4-22. The middle rails for one track route remain connected by the metal plate, while the middle rails for the other route are connected by the jumper wire soldered across the gap.

siding that doubles as a second, shorter loop. There is a station serving this line, along with three assorted freight handlers (fig. 4-23).

The el can be built atop fourteen 111 elevated trestles, with a station platform at each end and scratchbuilt staircases or elevator shafts to simulate access from street level. Because coffee table layouts are so small, choose tiny motive power for this line, perhaps a Lionel 60 trolley or a Bowser Birney. Using a more typical urban coach, such as a Budd-style car, is possible, though it's too large to look convincing on such a short

## THE EL

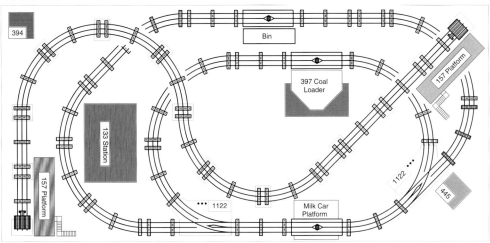

**Fig. 4-23**

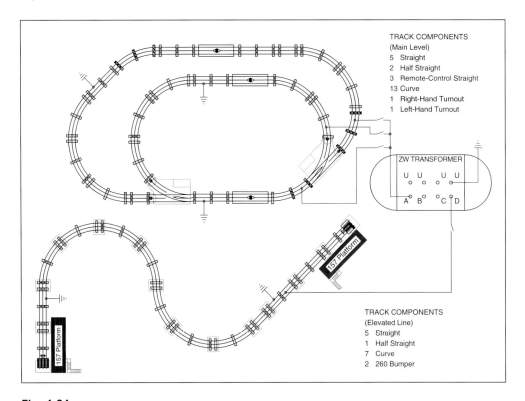

**Fig. 4-24**

see Metropolitan Transit and Interurban Rapid Transit in Chapter 6.)

For the main line, you'll need three wiring blocks: one for the section between the two turnouts and one for each loop (fig. 4-24). This arrangement lets you operate one train on either of the loops while a second one stands stationary on the other loop. The elevated line has its own throttle. If you don't have a transformer with two throttles, use a small separate transformer to power the trolley. (Another elevated line concept, Interurban, appears in Chapter 5.)

The coffee table layout offers the opportunity for a large amount of detail in a small place, with room for a surprising number of buildings and accessories, if you use a relatively simple track plan. Conversely, with the sharp curves of O27 track, a lot of operation can be packed into this limited area, but at the cost of scenic detail.

Of course, it doesn't take much more space to combine interesting operation with a satis-

run. The Lionel trolley is probably the best choice, as it reverses automatically upon striking the bumpers at each end. (For two more automatic reversing options, fying number of accessories. The next chapter looks at island layouts and begins with a design that's only twice the size of a coffee table railroad.

# 5

# MODULAR ISLAND LAYOUTS

An island layout is one that is accessible from all sides and typically stands in the middle of a room. Each of the designs in this chapter is based on 3'0" x 6'8" modules, some of which can be used alone or combined with one or two other modules according to the amount of space that's available.

The layout shown in fig. 5-1 is built on two 36" hollow-core doors for an overall surface dimension of 6'0" x 6'8", plus another inch in each direction to accommodate whatever molding you use along the edges. Any average room can absorb this layout, with space left over for some additional furniture.

The U-shaped track plan provides two possibilities for continuous running: the loop on the upper table and the loop at left that bridges both tables. In addition, there is a reverse loop at the lower right and another one at the upper right. These enable a train to travel continuously around the perimeter of the layout.

I've specified two town centers, one inside each reverse loop, as well as a residential area inside the left loop. This gives the trains logical departure and destination points. To provide some feeling of separation between the two towns, a low hill with appropriate trees and maybe a cliff or two spans the tables at the right center. Note that the hill is removable. One of the advantages of using hollow-core doors as modules is the option of enlarging the layout by inserting an extra

table or two. I describe this process later in the chapter.

One of the advantages of an island layout is visibility from every angle, and this layout features a lot of action for observers. There are several suggested locations for operating accessories, again to give the railroad a purpose. An engineer can deliver barrels, logs, or milk, and pick up sawed lumber and more barrels, as well as

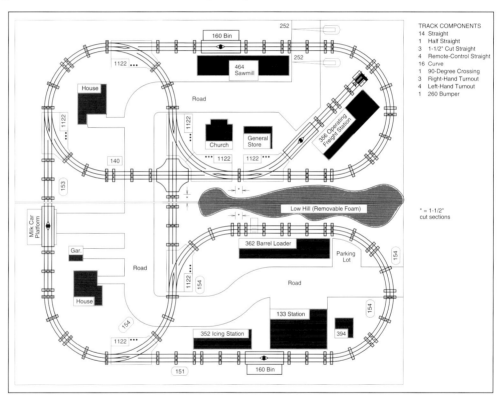

Fig. 5-1

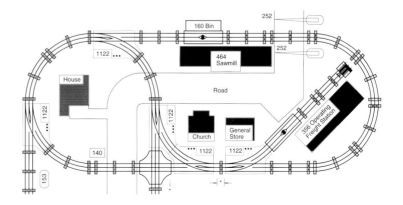

Fig. 5-2

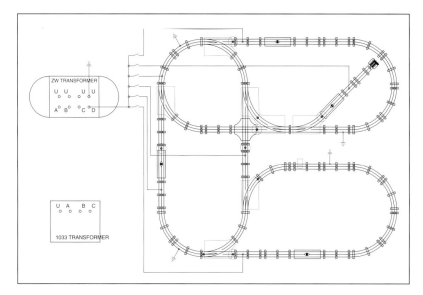

**Fig. 5-3**

## ELECTRICAL CONTROL

One of the throttles (post D) of the ZW transformer powers the track. Note the position of the fiber pins in the middle rail (fig. 5-3), especially at the junction of the two tables. This allows a modeler to operate the upper table independently when the two tables are separated. Multiple-wire plugs carry the wiring connections between the tables, as is explained in Chapter 7. I've provided a toggle switch for each of the six blocks and spaced four ground connections around the layout, each of them connected to the outside running rail.

I used three circuits for accessories. First, I set a wire from post C of the ZW at 9 or 10 volts for the bulbs in buildings and street lamps. Then I attached the second wire from each of these bulbs to the ground loop. For clarity, I omitted these simple connections from the diagram.

Next, as shown in fig. 5-4, I phased and grounded together the transformers (post U of the ZW to post A of the 1033). Post U of the 1033 transformer is the variable-voltage post, and it is controlled by the throttle handle. I use this post for accessories that operate in response to passing trains because using the separate transformer won't cause the trains to slow down. Even better, this arrangement enables you to adjust the voltage to a point where the crossing gates operate at a realistically slow speed. This circuit also feeds the 154 highway warning flasher, 153 block signal, and 140 banjo

load blocks of ice for refrigerated shipments. Luggage carts travel busily around the 356 operating freight station. A rotating beacon warns aircraft. (You may substitute other accessories, such as coal loaders or a diesel fueling station.) A roadway provides a reason for crossing gates and warning flashers, and I've added a store and a church for the inhabitants.

To return to the modular concept, you can build this layout with detachable connections between the tables and folding legs (see Chapter 7 for construction details). Note that if you remove the lower table, you can operate the upper table by itself (fig. 5-2), as it contains a continuous loop. This is a great advantage if you need to use the layout room for other activities. In addition, you can remove half of the layout, stand it on end for storage, and still run trains on the resulting 3'0" x 6'8" layout, leaving the rest of the room free when the extra space is needed.

It is visually desirable to have some open space between the track and the table edge. You can use this area for scenic devices, such as telephone poles, trees, and even an extra beacon or two. The O27 track shown in the diagram allows for this extra room, but the tables are large enough for O gauge track instead. If you favor bigger locomotives and rolling stock, the wider O gauge curves will allow their use, although they reduce the amount of table area around the perimeter of the track.

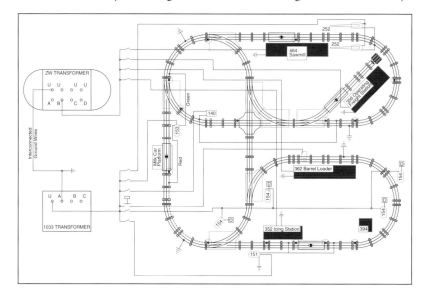

**Fig. 5-4**

signal, along with the OTC contactor for the barrel car, through a push button. (I explain the connections for these items in Chapter 1.)

I relied on post B of the ZW for the larger operating accessories. Since they're generally used when the trains are standing still, their current draw won't affect the speed of any of the locomotives. A toggle switch controls each accessory. You could use push buttons instead, but they require you to hold them down the entire time an accessory is operating.

## AN ADDITION

Just as you can halve a two-table island layout when space is at a premium, you can augment it when more of the room is available (such as when the kids are away at college). Figure 5-5 shows another 3'0" x 6'8" table inserted lengthwise between the first two. I removed the forested hill that spanned the two adjacent tables. The greater length of the main line makes travel between the two towns more realistic, and there's room for additional scenery and accessories.

I had to shorten a few pieces of the sectional track so they would fit properly; the approximate dimensions are shown on the plan, but they should be test-fit before you make the final cutting. Over such a long distance, even slight variations in the fit between track sections can alter the length of these special sections. When you're absolutely sure how long they must be, cut them with a hacksaw. Place the track section between a pair of flat, fabric-padded boards, and clamp it in a vise firmly enough to hold it, yet not so hard as to bend the rails. Use a new fine-toothed blade and short, gentle strokes. Bearing down hard or trying to cut too quickly distorts the rails. (If you're building this plan as a permanent layout, without the requirement that the tables come apart, the ends of the track sections need not end exactly at the edges of the doors. In this case it isn't necessary to shorten any sections of track.)

In addition to the two main lines, I added a passing siding at left, located at just the proper distance to accommodate one or both of the large prewar/early

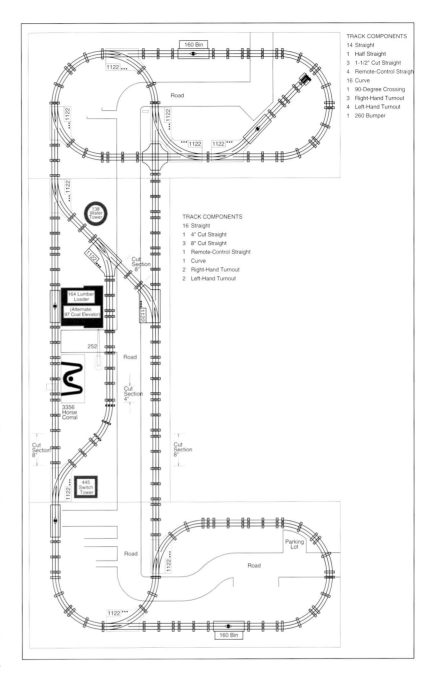

Fig. 5-5

postwar accessories, the 97 coal elevator and 164 lumber loader. Lionel designed these toys to receive freight on one side, from an appropriate dump car on an uncouple/unload ramp, and to deliver it on the other, making a siding such as this necessary for full operation. I've shown only one accessory on the plan, but there's room for both if you eliminate the roadway and move the 3356 horse corral closer to the lower turnout. (Lionel LLC has reissued the lumber loader, one of the most popular and fascinating of all postwar accessories.)

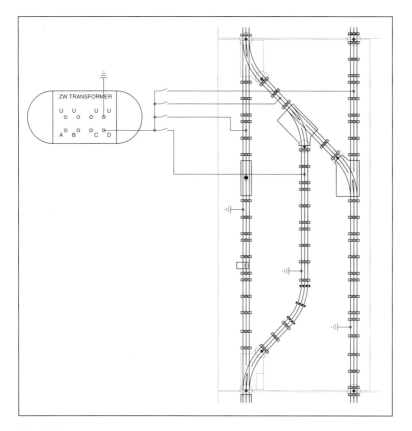

**Fig. 5-6**

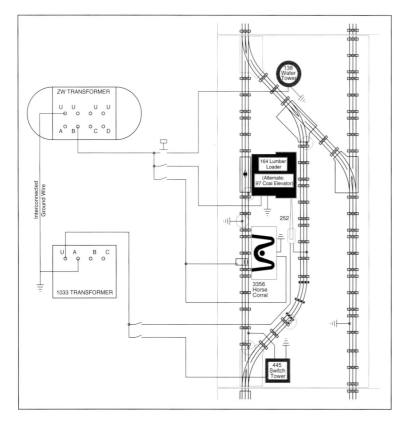

**Fig. 5-7**

The horse corral (or alternatively a 3656 cattle corral) makes an ideal choice for a narrow table such as this, since it's best viewed at close range. This portion of the layout also contains a water tower, 445 switch tower, and 252 crossing gate. A highway connects the two towns, although you can omit it if you wish to create the illusion that the towns are served primarily by the railroad. A crossover track between the two main lines provides another reverse loop for the layout and gives the engineer more route options.

For simplicity, this table has just four electrical blocks, one for each of the two main lines, one for the passing siding, and one for the crossover. You could combine the latter two tracks, but doing so would eliminate the possibility of having a train stand idle on the siding while another uses the crossover. As before, I've provided toggle switches for each block and connected the tracks to the ground loop (fig. 5-6).

Accessory wiring is similarly straightforward (fig. 5-7). I connected the crossing gate and the switch tower to the 1033 transformer to prevent voltage drop to the track when they're operating. Then I wired the other accessories to adjustable post B of the ZW, set for 14 to 16 volts. Typically, the big freight loaders require higher voltage than does the corral, where a full 16 volts can almost make the horses jump the fence. Since these accessories generally are used one at a time, you'll find that adjusting the voltage individually for each one is easy.

## VARIATIONS

As I mentioned in Chapter 1, the layouts in Lionel catalogs (especially the earlier issues) were mostly symmetrical in appearance. While not reflective of the real world, this balance is often desirable for a toy train layout, because it makes efficient use of the available space. You can minimize the mirror-image effect by using a variety of scenic details and accessories. Such a plan is shown in fig. 5-8.

This layout boasts three complete track loops, two of which are independent. You can run two trains simultaneously without ever crossing paths. A train can also circle the loop at left that spans both tables. Note that there are no reverse loops. If a train leaves one loop to circle another, it must back up to return to the point of origin. This is either an inconvenience or an opportunity for extra operation, depending on whether you like to run the trains continuously or prefer to stop, start, and reverse them more often. Reverse loops take up a lot of space, and eliminating them allows room for more operating accessories.

I provided two sidings as well as suggested locations for seven remote-control uncouple/unload ramps. At least six large trackside accessories (log, culvert, coal, and barrel loaders, for example) can occupy the central area, along with a milk car platform at far left. If you like a lot of accessories without crowding out all other kinds of scenery, this layout fills the bill.

Wiring is simple, with a block for each principal loop and a block for each siding. For independent control of two trains, run the wires for the upper loop and siding to throttle post D of the ZW and the wires for the lower loop and siding to throttle post A. With this variation, when a train is running on the left-hand loop that spans both tables, you can control it alternately by the

two throttle handles, A and D, according to which table it is on at any given moment. If you don't plan to operate two trains at one time, all tracks may be wired to one throttle.

Adding the extra table shown in fig. 5-9 provides reverse capability as well as more storage sidings and extra scenery and accessory space. Note that any train leaving one of the outer loops and entering the central table will cross over to the opposite main line. Upon reaching the other loop, it will be oriented so that it can leave that loop at any time without backing up.

In this installation, the central table is wired to throttle post U of a 1033 transformer. This allows an engineer to operate a locomotive on the central table while two other trains circle the loops unaffected and unattended. I interconnected the ZW and the 1033 by their ground posts and phased them with respect to the house current. (The diagram also shows another 1033, which is reserved for accessories.)

If you don't have a second transformer, you can wire the tracks on the middle table to post B or C of the ZW. The voltage produced by these two posts is variable, although lacking whistle and direction controls. Using

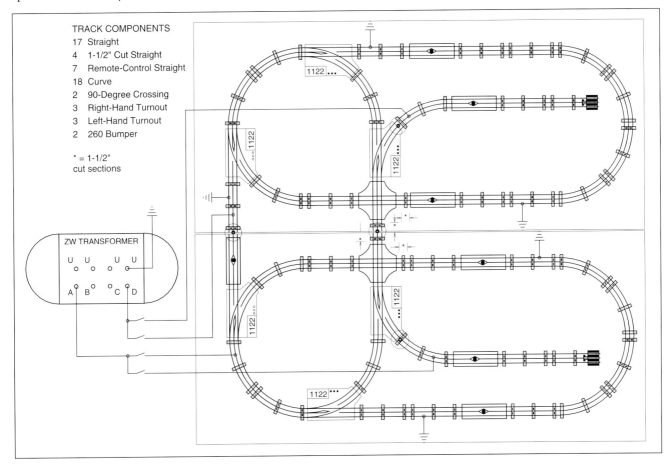

TRACK COMPONENTS

17 Straight
4 1-1/2" Cut Straight
7 Remote-Control Straight
18 Curve
2 90-Degree Crossing
3 Right-Hand Turnout
3 Left-Hand Turnout
2 260 Bumper

* = 1-1/2"
cut sections

ZW TRANSFORMER

**Fig. 5-8**

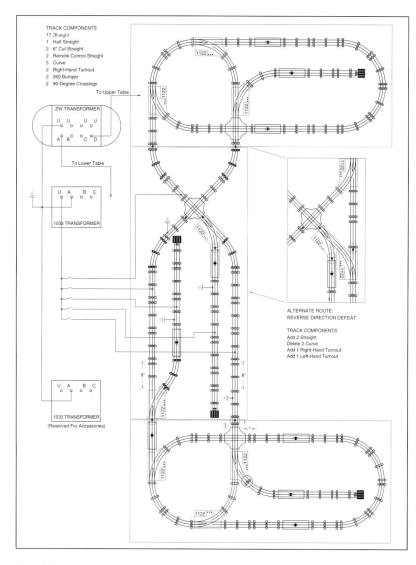

TRACK COMPONENTS
17 Straight
1 Half Straight
2 8" Cut Straight
2 Remote Control Straight
5 Curve
2 Right-Hand Turnout
2 260 Bumper
2 90-Degree Crossings

To Upper Table

ZW TRANSFORMER
U U U U
A B C D

To Lower Table

U A B C
1033 TRANSFORMER

ALTERNATE ROUTE:
REVERSE DIRECTION DEFEAT

TRACK COMPONENTS
Add 2 Straight
Delete 2 Curve
Add 1 Right-Hand Turnout
Add 1 Left-Hand Turnout

U A B C
1033 TRANSFORMER
(Reserved For Accessories)

8"

8"

**Fig. 5-9**

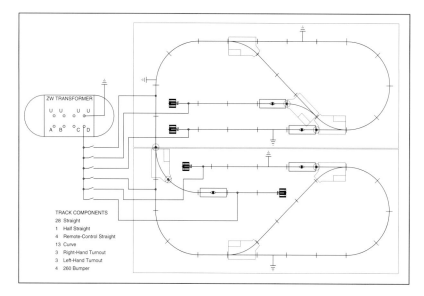

ZW TRANSFORMER
U U U U
A B C D

TRACK COMPONENTS
28 Straight
1 Half Straight
4 Remote-Control Straight
13 Curve
3 Right-Hand Turnout
3 Left-Hand Turnout
4 260 Bumper

**Fig. 5-10**

B or C as a throttle, however, means it can't be used for accessories.

With this track plan, a train will *always* reverse direction when passing over the middle table. By adding an extra pair of switches, an operator has the option of avoiding this direction reversal, as shown in the insert. There are also two stub sidings, each with a remote-control uncoupling track. You can use these sidings for storing rolling stock or for operating accessories. The locations of the remote-control ramps are optional. When placed as shown, they enable an operator to leave a string of cars on the sidings; if placed in front of a log loader, saw mill, or similar accessory, they can be used as needed.

## TWO TABLES

Each of the modular layouts discussed to this point provides for continuous operation in a minimum amount of space by having at least one complete loop entirely on a single table. If you have enough room for two tables to be up at all times (an area 6'0" x 6'8"), track planning becomes less restrictive.

Figure 5-10 is a nearly symmetrical layout with a reverse loop and a pair of sidings on each table. There's enough room for a variety of accessories located along the stub sidings, along with a few buildings and scenery within the loops. The suggested wiring features two mainline blocks (one per table) and a block for each siding. As was the case with the first layout in this chapter (fig. 5-1), you can place a low hill or another scenic barrier across the joint between the tables.

Figure 5-11 is the same basic layout, only it features an additional pair of turnouts (shown at right) that allow a train to circle the perimeter. In return for the increased operational variety, there's a slight penalty in terms of realism. In the previous design, a train is *required* to use the reverse loops, and locating a town at each loop gives a train the illusion of a departure point and a destination. The extra two turnouts provide an escape route, though they compromise the purpose of the original track plan. If you enjoy watching your trains circle the table, this option may appeal to you. (You can disguise it somewhat by locating a small hill with a tunnel at this point.)

These extra turnouts allow some interesting options, however, if you insert a third table between the original two (fig. 5-12). The towns are further separated, with interesting scenic possibilities in the central area, and trains have a much longer run between stations.

As shown, a crossover is hidden beneath a mountain, which has four tunnel portals. Even though the layout is symmetrical, the two reverse loops allow a variety of different patterns of operation. The mountain creates an illusion of distance, but even without it, the layout is interesting to watch. If space is at a premium, make the middle table removable.

The geometry of sectional track doesn't quite work out for this design. Although the 36"-wide door is a perfect size for O27 track, with its 9"-long straight sections, the diameter of the curves at right prevents the two middle tracks from being exactly parallel. They will be slightly wider apart

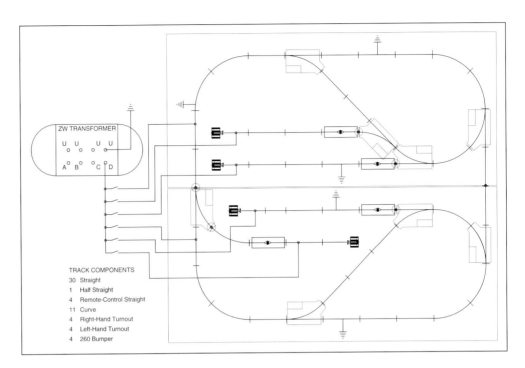

TRACK COMPONENTS
30   Straight
1    Half Straight
4    Remote-Control Straight
11   Curve
4    Right-Hand Turnout
4    Left-Hand Turnout
4    260 Bumper

**Fig. 5-11**

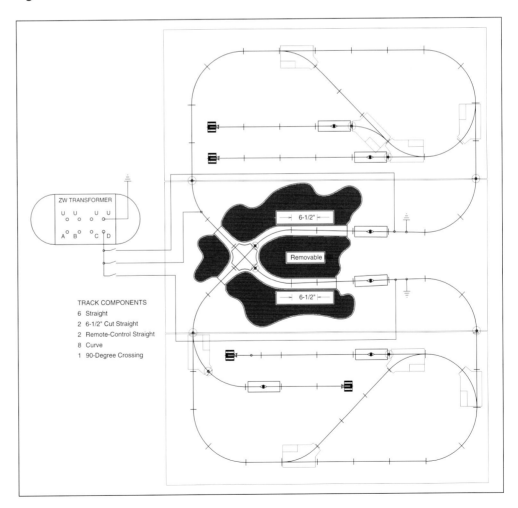

TRACK COMPONENTS
6   Straight
2   6-1/2" Cut Straight
2   Remote-Control Straight
8   Curve
1   90-Degree Crossing

**Fig. 5-12**

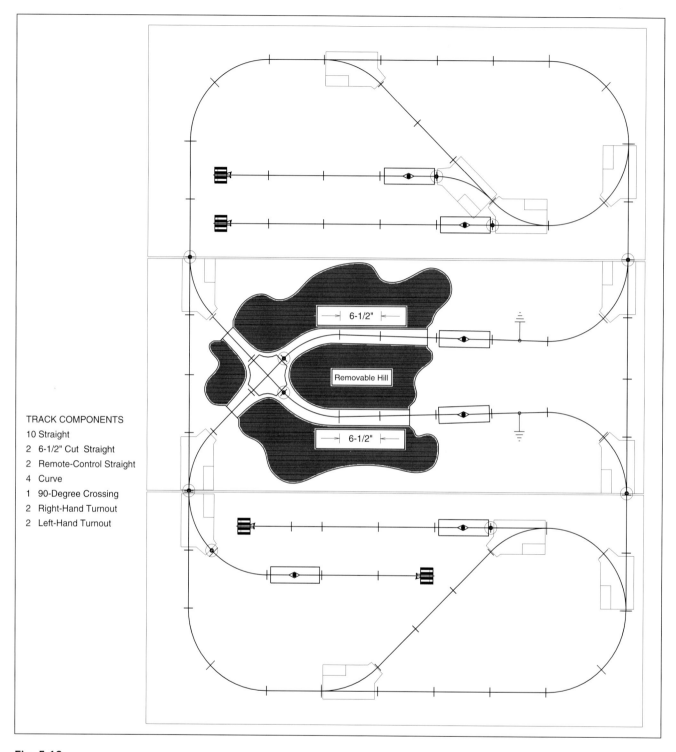

TRACK COMPONENTS
10 Straight
2　6-1/2" Cut　Straight
2　Remote-Control Straight
4　Curve
1　90-Degree Crossing
2　Right-Hand Turnout
2　Left-Hand Turnout

6-1/2"

6-1/2"

Removable Hill

**Fig. 5-13**

where they emerge from the 90-degree crossing than they are at the right. However, you can angle sectional track slightly to compensate for this difference without adversely affecting operation. In addition, you must shorten a couple of sections to 6½" to fit properly (fig. 5-12).

Four more turnouts (two right-hand and two left-hand) allow a rectangular loop around the entire layout (fig. 5-13). This greatly increases the number of routes a train may take. If operation is your goal and you don't care about the illusion of logical destination points, you'll find that this plan has lots of possibilities.

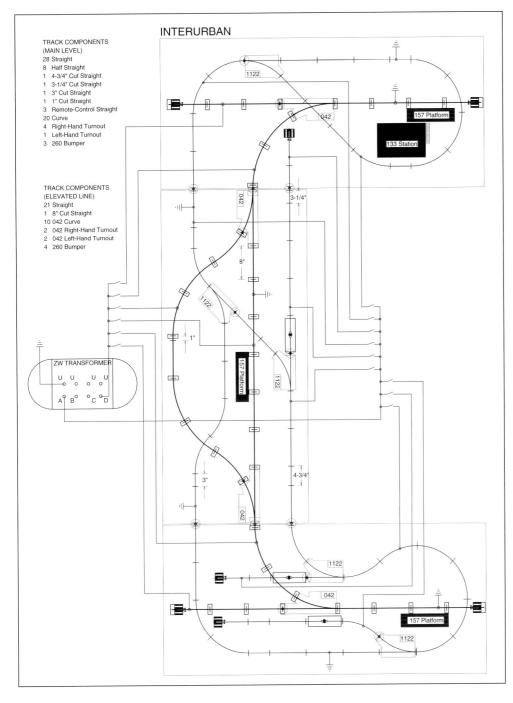

INTERURBAN

TRACK COMPONENTS
(MAIN LEVEL)
28 Straight
8 Half Straight
1 4-3/4" Cut Straight
1 3-1/4" Cut Straight
1 3" Cut Straight
1 1" Cut Straight
3 Remote-Control Straight
20 Curve
4 Right-Hand Turnout
1 Left-Hand Turnout
3 260 Bumper

TRACK COMPONENTS
(ELEVATED LINE)
21 Straight
1 8" Cut Straight
10 042 Curve
2 042 Right-Hand Turnout
2 042 Left-Hand Turnout
4 260 Bumper

ZW TRANSFORMER

157 Platform

133 Station

157 Platform

**Fig. 5-14**

## INTERURBAN

If you favor city-like buildings and scenery, you may want to add an elevated passenger line. As shown in fig. 5-14, you arrange three tables in the shape of a U, with a main line and a reverse loop at each end for freight service. There are three storage sidings and enough room for numerous accessories and buildings, although only one (a 133 station at upper right) is shown. The other accessories are optional, depending upon your imagination.

Passenger service is provided by the elevated line (el) that you build atop 41 Lionel 111 trestles. These track supports were sold in sets of ten and have been reissued in recent years under catalog number 2755; you will need five sets. I've shown double trestles at the joints between the tables. If you plan to connect the tables permanently, you can omit these doubles. Then you will need only 39 trestle bents (four 111 sets).

In addition, you also can use wide O42 curves, which accommodate Lionel's Budd cars (a reasonable approximation of modern interurban cars). (You can substitute regular O31 curves, but the big Budd cars look especially awkward on an elevated line with such sharp turns.) You also may want to use a 60 trolley or even the recently produced Lackawanna or Pennsylvania M.U. cars. Whatever motive power you choose, be sure it's double-ended, as the el has no reverse loops.

I located a 157 station platform at each end of the line and at one intermediate stop and raised these accessories to the level of the el tracks. Between the 157 and the 133 stations at the upper right I placed a stairway to give passengers access to the trains. I also added a spur siding at each end for storing extra cars.

The wiring diagram provides control of the freight line with throttle A and the el line with throttle D. Automatic station stops and reversing are possible, using a Lionel stop station or electronic circuits.

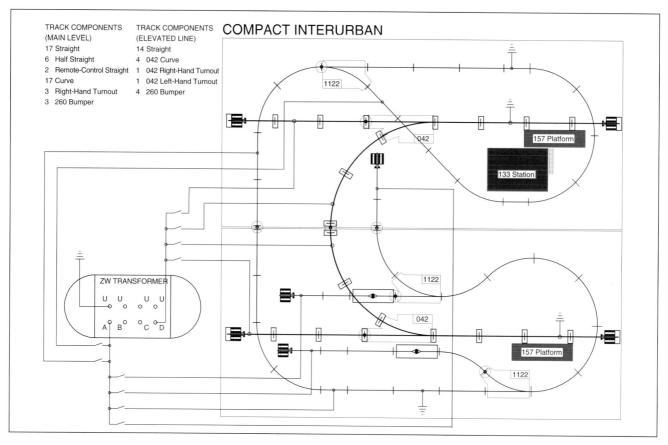

Fig. 5-15

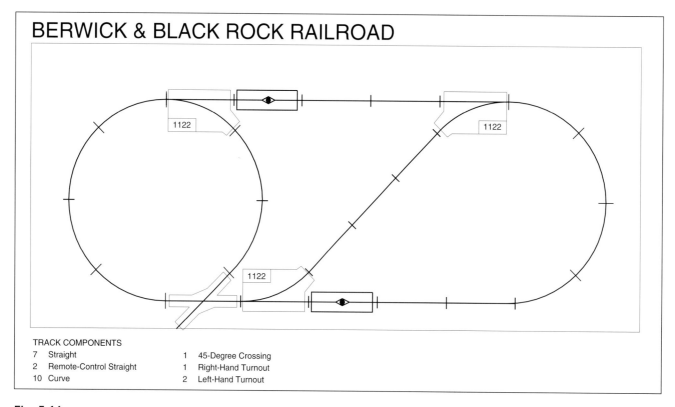

Fig. 5-16

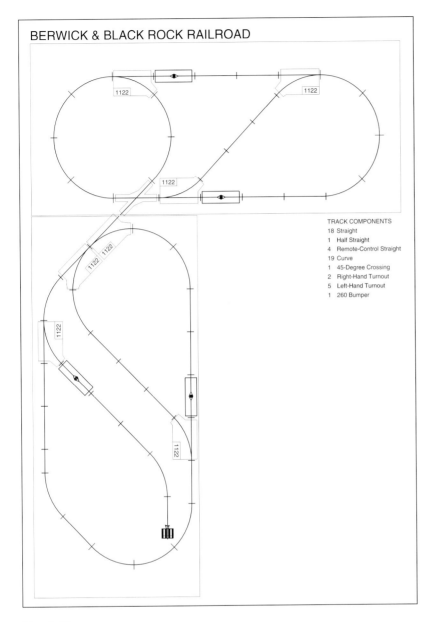

BERWICK & BLACK ROCK RAILROAD

TRACK COMPONENTS
18  Straight
1   Half Straight
4   Remote-Control Straight
19  Curve
1   45-Degree Crossing
2   Right-Hand Turnout
5   Left-Hand Turnout
1   260 Bumper

**Fig. 5-17**

instead of 41. Aside from having a short el line, this layout has the twin disadvantages of compact spur sidings and no second reverse loop on the freight line. The best choice of motive power would be small switchers (NW2 or shorter) that would pull or push trains consisting of only two or three cars.

## BERWICK & BLACK ROCK RAILROAD

Depending upon the shape of the area available for a layout, you can arrange modular tables in a variety of patterns. With a little ingenuity, you can modify any of these layouts to fit. As an example, the Berwick & Black Rock Railroad uses the same three tables as the previous designs, though in a slightly altered pattern.

The first table (fig. 5-16) has a loop with a reverse loop and a nearly complete circle that exits through a 45-degree crossing. You can use this part of the layout alone, and there is room for a variety of scenery or accessories. I've located the crossing at the lower edge of the table, which provides extra space along the opposite edge for such accessories as a 362 barrel loader, 364 log loader, or 464 sawmill.

The second table attaches at the site of the 45-degree crossing and also contains a continuous loop with a reverse loop, along with a stub siding (fig. 5-17). By wiring the two tables to separate throttles, you can have trains circling the two loops independently, or a single train can travel back and forth along the entire main line, using the two reverse loops. This provides an exceptionally long run for such a small layout. Finally, you can operate this second table by itself.

You can create a larger layout by detaching the second table and inserting the third between the first two (fig. 5-18). Note that the table arrangement is different from previous designs, creating an asymmetrical U-shaped layout. The central table has a reverse loop and a stub siding, but no continuous loop. There's ample room for scenery and accessories, along with an exceptionally long run for a train over the entire main line, thanks to the placement of the reverse loops. You

Chapter 6 discusses these components and their use, under the headings Metropolitan Transit and Interurban Rapid Transit.

In a manner similar to the other layouts in this chapter, I've designed the Interurban to be symmetrical so you can omit the central table for operation in a small space (fig. 5-15). This variation is less successful visually than the earlier designs, however, as the distance traveled by the el trains will be too short to be realistic. Nevertheless, if you want an el and are limited to a small layout room, you'll find this solution worth investigating.

If you have to disconnect the tables, be sure you use paired trestle bents at the table joints. The compact two-table version needs only 24 trestles (three 111 sets), can model three towns, each located inside one of the reverse loops.

Figure 5-19 shows a two-throttle wiring pattern that allows for independent control of the two continuous loops. In addition, you can attach the middle table to either throttle, to post B or C, or to a second transformer.

Each of the foregoing designs relies on the modular concept, allowing one or two tables to be omitted while still preserving some operation. The track patterns therefore are somewhat symmetrical. As Chapter 6 explains, less restrictive island layouts, which are built without this take-apart feature, allow for more imaginative track plans.

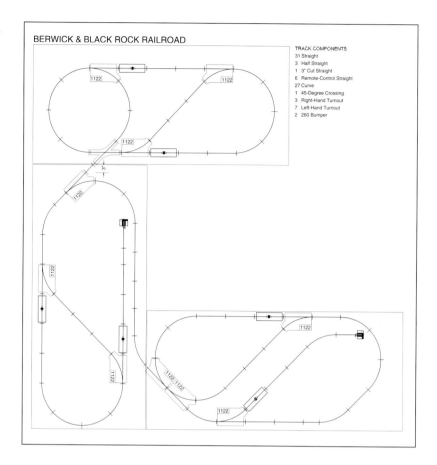

BERWICK & BLACK ROCK RAILROAD

TRACK COMPONENTS
31 Straight
3 Half Straight
1 3" Cut Straight
6 Remote-Control Straight
27 Curve
1 45-Degree Crossing
3 Right-Hand Turnout
7 Left-Hand Turnout
2 260 Bumper

**Fig. 5-18**

**Fig. 5-19**

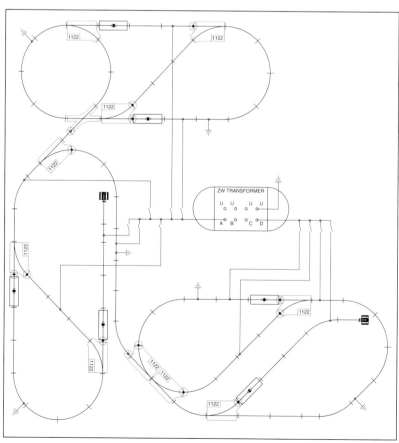

ZW TRANSFORMER

# INDIVISIBLE ISLAND LAYOUTS

Three-foot-wide hollow-core doors make ideal train tables for a variety of reasons, some of which I addressed in previous chapters. Not to be overlooked is the matter of an operator's arm reach, as 3 feet is close to the maximum comfortable working distance for most people. Two doors placed side by side make a 6-foot-wide layout, with plenty of room for lots of track and accessories yet easily accessible from both sides for building and maintenance.

Adding a third table across the ends of two such tables gives an effective layout area of 6'0" x 9'8". As layouts increase in size, you need more and more space for the control panel. Aligning three tables in this manner provides an extra 8 inches for the transformers and other controls.

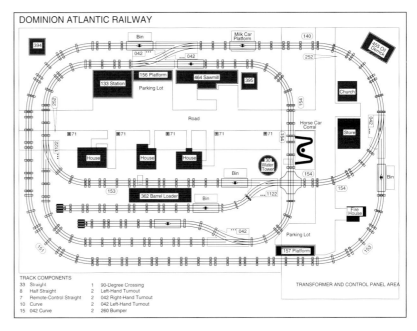

Fig. 6-1

## MULTI-INDUSTRY DESIGN

For a modeler seeking to incorporate a wide variety of accessories, three doors afford ample room. The Dominion Atlantic Railway (named after a branch of the Canadian Pacific in Nova Scotia) shows how you can include four or more industries while still leaving room for homes and a small commercial district (fig. 6-1).

This layout avoids the temptation to fill every available inch with track, yet provides lots of operational possibilities. I reserved the upper central area for a highway and residential area and situated a town center at the right. Widely spaced stations offer passenger destinations, and various freight and livestock handlers give plenty of action. (As with previous layouts, builders are free to substitute favorite accessories for those shown in the diagram.) You can store rolling stock on two sidings. Adding more sidings is possible, though doing so would mean the elimination of some scenic details and structures.

You'll find there's room for a suburban station and three houses with generous yards surrounding them. If you choose a town house appearance, you can double this number. Five 71 lampposts line the highway, and there are several grade crossings that need gates, warning flashers, or other devices, such as the 140 banjo

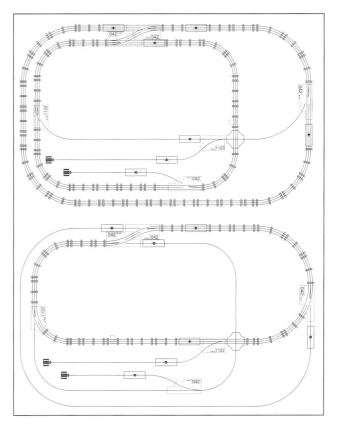

Fig. 6-2

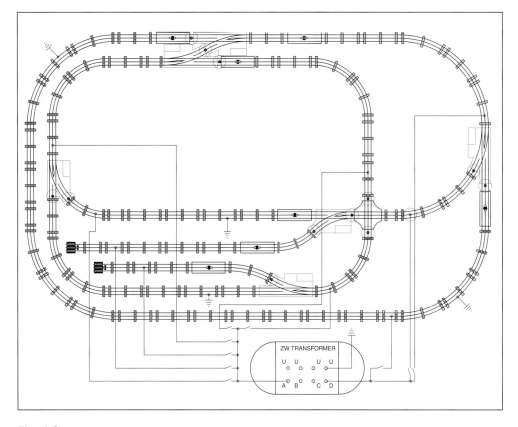

**Fig. 6-3**

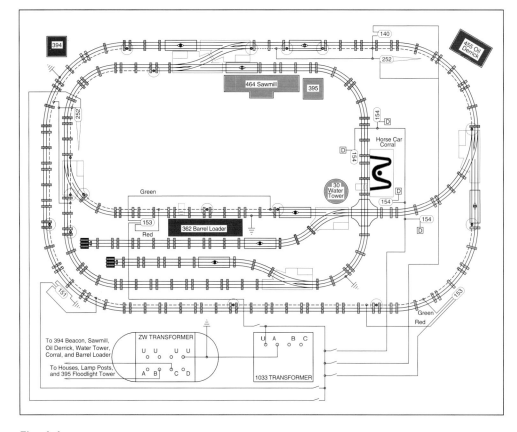

**Fig. 6-4**

signal at the upper right. The town has suggested locations for a church, store, firehouse and station platform, and you can try to squeeze in more buildings as well as additional lamp posts.

Using O42 gauge curves on the outer loop and O27 on the inner makes possible the double-track main line. The geometry isn't correct for exactly consistent spacing between the tracks around the curves, but this does not detract from the appearance of a small layout such as this. For exact concentric curves, consider using flexible track or the intermediate sectional track sizes, currently on the market from several manufacturers.

The tracks of the inner loop won't be exactly parallel because the crossover is slightly shorter than a regular section of O27 track. Fortunately, sectional track can accommodate such slight variations. Should this one bother you, however, cut a very short section of straight track and insert it between the crossing and the curved section below it.

Continuous independent operation of two trains is possible on the two mainline loops, as shown in one of the diagrams in fig. 6-2. There is another continuous loop, which makes

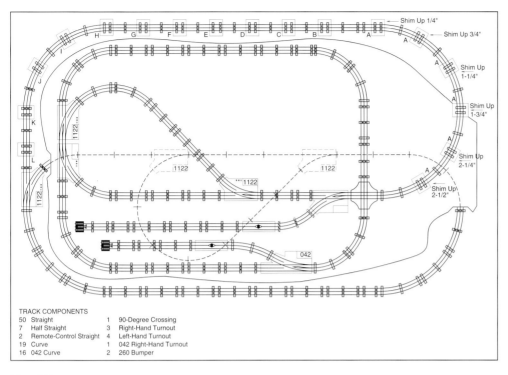

**Fig. 6-5**

TRACK COMPONENTS

| | | | |
|---|---|---|---|
| 50 | Straight | 1 | 90-Degree Crossing |
| 7 | Half Straight | 3 | Right-Hand Turnout |
| 2 | Remote-Control Straight | 4 | Left-Hand Turnout |
| 19 | Curve | 1 | 042 Right-Hand Turnout |
| 16 | 042 Curve | 2 | 260 Bumper |

use of parts of the other two. While one train is operating on this route, others can sit stationary in blocks on the other loops, shown as single-line tracks.

Figure 6-3 shows the blocks. Throttle D of the ZW transformer controls the outer loop, and throttle A runs the inner one and the sidings. Operating on the combination loop (fig. 6-2, lower diagram) requires switching from one throttle to the other as the train crosses the turnouts. Note that I've arranged the blocks so that power can be shut off to those sections of track that aren't needed for the combination loop. In theory, three trains could be present on the layout at all times. Even more would be possible, but too many trains present a crowded appearance and may make operation difficult. With too many trains, no matter where you wish to go, there always seems to be another train in the way.

Post B of the ZW is reserved for the lampposts, house lights, and 395 floodlight tower and should be set at a conservative level (10 to 11 volts) to give a realistic soft glow to these bulbs and to extend their lives. I don't show the connections for these accessories because

they're so simple. Just attach each bulb or accessory to the ground loop by one wire and to post B by the other wire. You can also include toggle switches to turn them off separately.

The 394 rotary beacon (upper left) is a heat-activated accessory and works best at higher voltage. For that reason I attached one wire to the ground loop and the other to a fixed post giving 16 volts, such as post C of the 1033 transformer. I omitted this simple connection from the diagram for clarity.

I wired the automatic accessories to variable-voltage post U of the 1033 (fig. 6-4), set to a voltage that works best for the crossing gates (13 to 14 volts). One power wire goes to each accessory; the other wire connects to insulated outside running rails as shown. As a

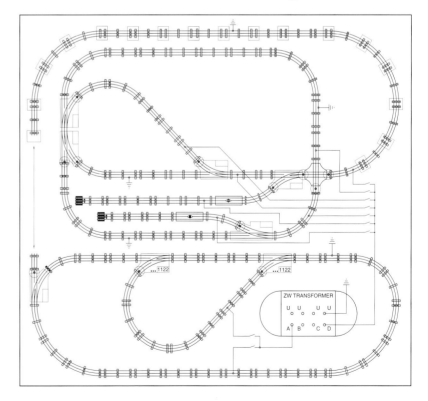

**Fig. 6-6**

train contacts each of these rails, it causes the gates to go down, the banjo signal to wag, the block signals to turn red or green, and the semaphore arm to lower. (The 151 semaphore has a supplementary ground connection that keeps its lamp illuminated at all times, even when the arm isn't operating.) You can connect the 154 high-way flashers to 154C contactors or through electronic flashers to insulated running rails, as described in previous chapters.

Next, I reserved post C of the ZW for the operating accessories: sawmill, water tower, barrel loader, oil derrick, and horse corral. A setting of about 14 volts should work well for these items, although you may wish to adjust the output when operating the horse corral if the livestock tries to jump the fence and gallop off into the sunset!

## TWO-LEVEL LAYOUT

If your locomotives have Magne-Traction or if you pull short, lightweight trains, you can alter this layout by using parts from a 110 graduated trestle set and a 111 elevated trestle set. As shown in fig. 6-5, the central area of the layout is raised almost 8 inches. The outer loop no longer circles the perimeter of the tables, although it seems to. Instead, there is a partially hidden loop with a reverse loop under the mountain. The graduated trestle sections (L through B) raise the track to a height of about 5 inches, and the elevated sections (A) are shimmed to complete the grade. The resulting height of 8 inches allows sufficient room beneath the mountain for large equipment and is high enough to allow you to use Lionel tunnel portals.

The upper portion of the layout is almost unchanged from the

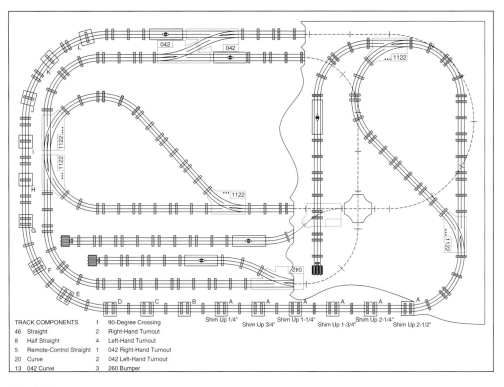

| TRACK COMPONENTS | | 1 | 90-Degree Crossing |
|---|---|---|---|
| 46 | Straight | 2 | Right-Hand Turnout |
| 8 | Half Straight | 4 | Left-Hand Turnout |
| 5 | Remote-Control Straight | 1 | 042 Right-Hand Turnout |
| 20 | Curve | 2 | 042 Left-Hand Turnout |
| 13 | 042 Curve | 3 | 260 Bumper |

**Fig. 6-7**

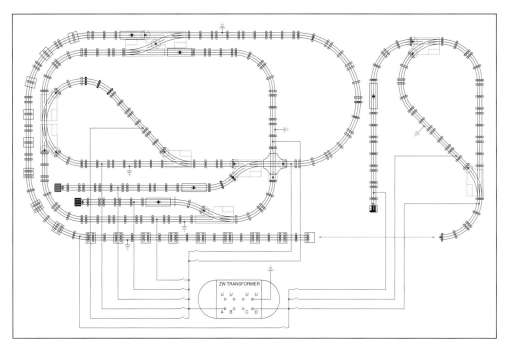

**Fig. 6-8**

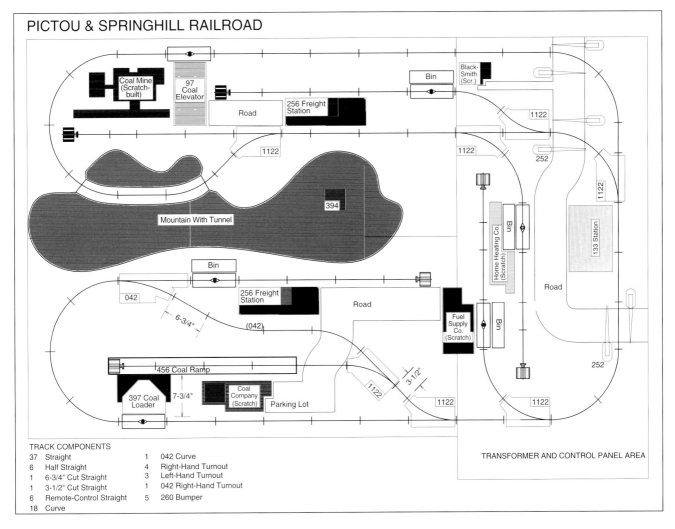

**PICTOU & SPRINGHILL RAILROAD**

TRACK COMPONENTS

| | | | |
|---|---|---|---|
| 37 | Straight | 1 | 042 Curve |
| 6 | Half Straight | 4 | Right-Hand Turnout |
| 1 | 6-3/4" Cut Straight | 3 | Left-Hand Turnout |
| 1 | 3-1/2" Cut Straight | 1 | 042 Right-Hand Turnout |
| 6 | Remote-Control Straight | 5 | 260 Bumper |
| 18 | Curve | | |

**Fig. 6-9**

previous version, except that I've added a reverse loop. The two reverse loops (upper and lower) allow a train always to travel between the levels in the forward direction. You can eliminate these loops if you don't mind backing up or down the mountain.

Fewer buildings are possible with this design, but the additional scenic effects possible with a bilevel layout compensate for this lack. I recommend locating a station and any operating accessories on the upper level and placing at least one station platform on the lower level, possibly at the lower right. You can situate other items in the unused corners of the table.

Figure 6-6 shows suggested wiring blocks, with throttle D connected to the

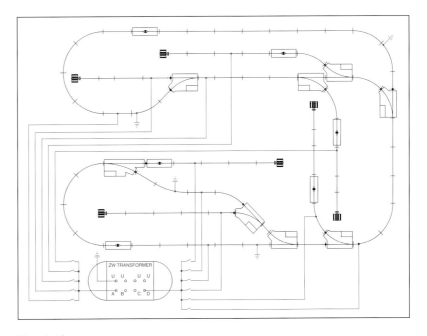

**Fig. 6-10**

## THE BLUEBERRY EXPRESS

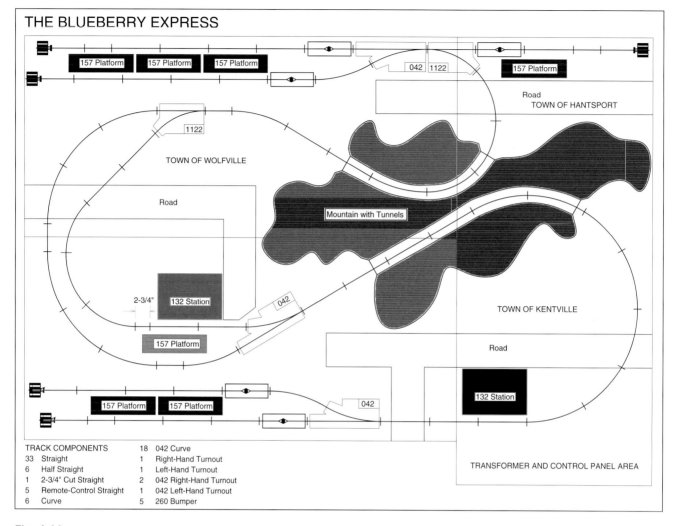

| TRACK COMPONENTS | | 18 | 042 Curve |
|---|---|---|---|
| 33 | Straight | 1 | Right-Hand Turnout |
| 6 | Half Straight | 1 | Left-Hand Turnout |
| 1 | 2-3/4" Cut Straight | 2 | 042 Right-Hand Turnout |
| 5 | Remote-Control Straight | 1 | 042 Left-Hand Turnout |
| 6 | Curve | 5 | 260 Bumper |

**Fig. 6-11**

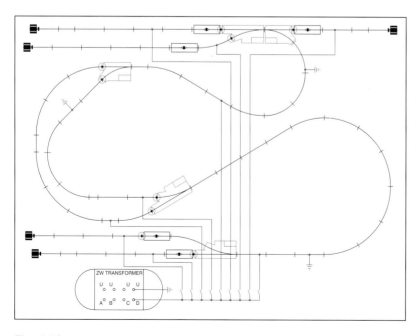

**Fig. 6-12**

upper level and throttle A to the lower one. You can connect lights and freight-handling accessories to posts B and C (as described above) and wire automatic accessories, such as crossing gates and gatemen, to a separate 1033 and insulated outside running rails (located where appropriate to the scenery).

By elevating all the central area of this layout on a plateau, you draw attention to a single town or city area, with the illusion of trains departing for distant locations through the tunnel portal at the lower right. By raising only about one-third of the layout, however, you create two town centers, one high and one low, and conduct freight and passenger services between the two. This concept is shown in fig. 6-7.

Once again, you need two reverse loops for bidirectional running up and down the hill. The lower portion of the layout is similar to the first design in this chapter. You can run trains continuously on the central rectangular loop or on the irregularly shaped loop highlighted in one of the diagrams of fig. 6-2.

This design features three storage sidings: one on the upper level and two below. Both levels can have complementary industries (operating accessories), such as a log loader down below and a sawmill up top. For example, you can model a coal mine with a 97 coal elevator on the upper level, and deliver the product to a coal yard (397 diesel-type coal loader) on the main level or substitute a 456 coal ramp for the longest siding. There are many other possibilities, limited only by your imagination.

I've divided the lower level into eight blocks and the upper one into four (including the hill) and then connected them to the two throttles of the ZW (fig. 6-8). You can connect accessories to posts B and C and to a separate 1033, according to the principles established in designs shown earlier in this book.

You can dump coal into the elevator at the remote-control track section (top left), but the main purpose of the structure is to load hoppers waiting on the siding on the elevator's opposite side.

The table at the bottom right is the primary destination for trains from the coal mine. I located a scratch-built coal company here. A locomotive backs hoppers

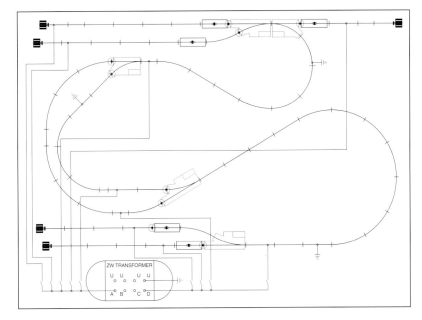

**Fig. 6-13**

## AN INDUSTRY-BASED LAYOUT

Many operators enjoy a layout with a concentration on one particular industry, with a track plan designed to serve the various aspects of this industry: production, delivery, and consumption. Such a layout is the Pictou & Springhill Railroad, set in the coal mining region of northern Nova Scotia (fig. 6-9).

On the table at the upper left, a 97 coal elevator is the central focus of a mining area. Naturally, you can scratch-build or kitbash additional structures that are associated with mining.

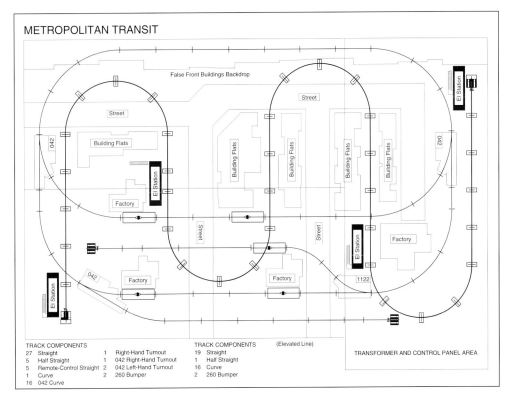

**Fig. 6-14**

coming from the mine onto the 456 coal ramp, where they unload into the 397 coal loader below. In turn, the 397 transfers the coal to low-sided dump cars, which then carry the coal to consumers located around the layout: a fuel supply company, a blacksmith, and a home heating company. You can situate additional "delivery locations" (trackside bins) wherever you'd like; I placed one to the left of the 256 freight station near the center of the layout.

The road that passes through the town center does not connect with either the coal company or the mine. This preserves the illusion that the railroad is the only means of distribution available to the industry. The mountain I erected in the center creates physical separation between the mine and the primary distributor.

Elsewhere, there are other accessories, including a 394 rotary beacon and various crossing gates; You can add more as desired. I wired these accessories and the lighted structures in the same manner as shown on previous layouts. Track wiring is straightforward, with one throttle controlling the upper mine area and the other handling the town and the coal company (fig. 6-10).

## THE *BLUEBERRY EXPRESS*

Prior to 1994, the Canadian Pacific operated passenger service on its Dominion Atlantic subsidiary between Yarmouth and Halifax, Nova Scotia, via the beautiful Annapolis Valley. Sadly, a lack of passengers forced cancellation of the service, and now the tracks for half of the line, the section between Kentville and Yarmouth, have been torn up.

For about two decades following the Second World War, steam locomotives pulled heavyweight coaches along this route, but as highways improved and the automobile became nearly ubiquitous, more economical motive power was needed. Like many other North American railroads, the Canadian Pacific turned to Rail Diesel Cars manufactured by the Budd Company, and for nearly three more decades these sleek silver coaches trundled through some of the most beautiful agricultural land in the world. In addition to its world-famous apple orchards, the Annapolis Valley boasts huge tracts of cultivated blueberry bushes, with many acres adjoining the rail line. The Budd RDCs soon became known locally as the *Blueberry Express.*

On its journey to Halifax, the *Blueberry Express* used to pass through the town of Kentville, where I live, then eastward through Wolfville (the home of my employer, Acadia University) and on to Hantsport. This section of the line serves as the inspiration for the passenger-only design that's shown in fig. 6-11.

I didn't include any reverse loops, as a Rail Diesel Car can operate equally well in either direction and need not be turned at the end of the line. I suggested station platforms for the two end-of-the-line locations and placed other stations in logical spots. Most of the line uses O42 curved track, since Lionel's Budd cars (such as the 18506 Canadian National models) look best on curves wider than O27. The single-track main line leaves

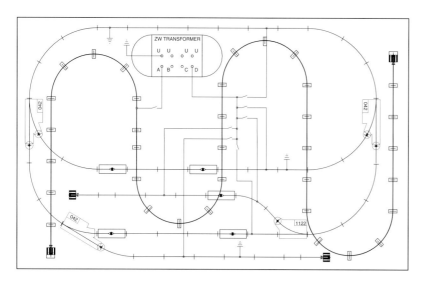

Fig. 6-15

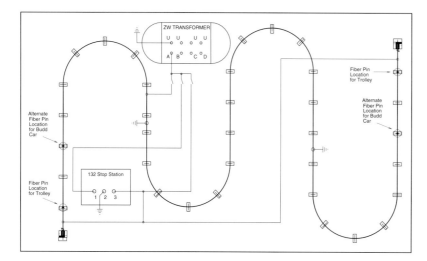

Fig. 6-16

room for a few buildings and other details in the towns, and a passing siding allows simultaneous operation of two RDCs running in opposite directions and passing each other in Wolfville.

I used a bit of artistic license for the tunnels through the mountain, since there are no railroad tunnels in the Annapolis Valley. The mountain is a scenic device to create a sense of separation between the towns. For the same reason, I didn't create any highway connections between the towns.

The easiest way to wire the layout is to divide it into nine blocks (fig. 6-12) connected to a single throttle. If you plan to operate two Budd trains in opposite directions, connect the Hantsport area and one of the Wolfville passing sidings to throttle A, and the other passing siding and the Kentville area to throttle D (fig. 6-13).

## METROPOLITAN TRANSIT

A three-door table is an ideal size for re-creating part of a small city, with ordinary rail service to manufacturing plants and an elevated rapid transit system. Although few of Lionel's accessories fit this concept, other manufacturers make a variety of kits and components of an urban nature. If you enjoy assembling structures and kitbashing, you should like this plan (fig. 6-14).

The main line is a simple loop, with a central passing siding and two industrial sidings. All curves and turnouts are O42, except for one O27 turnout and one O27 curve on the second siding up from the bottom of the diagram. To give the illusion of trains passing through the city to and from other locations, I erected a backdrop of false-front buildings that hides the back section of the loop.

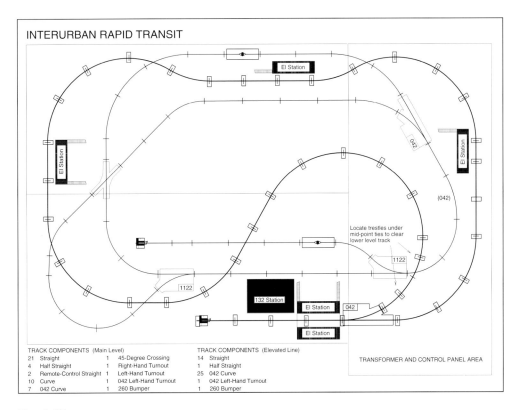

INTERURBAN RAPID TRANSIT

El Station

Locate trestles under mid-point ties to clear lower level track

132 Station

TRANSFORMER AND CONTROL PANEL AREA

| TRACK COMPONENTS (Main Level) | | | |
|---|---|---|---|
| 21 | Straight | 1 | 45-Degree Crossing |
| 4 | Half Straight | 1 | Right-Hand Turnout |
| 2 | Remote-Control Straight | 1 | Left-Hand Turnout |
| 10 | Curve | 1 | 042 Left-Hand Turnout |
| 7 | 042 Curve | 1 | 260 Bumper |

| TRACK COMPONENTS (Elevated Line) | | |
|---|---|---|
| 14 | Straight | |
| 1 | Half Straight | |
| 25 | 042 Curve | |
| 1 | 042 Left-Hand Turnout | |
| 1 | 260 Bumper | |

**Fig. 6-17**

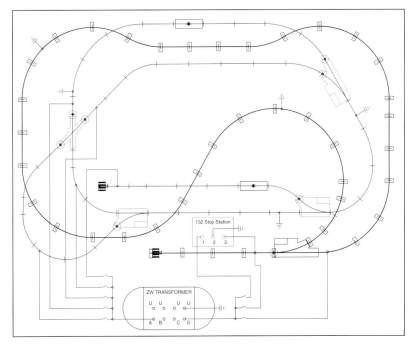

132 Stop Station

ZW TRANSFORMER

**Fig. 6-18**

Several types of modular commercial buildings are available for this purpose, from Design Preservation Models, among other manufacturers. If you want a less expensive approach, try using the printed cardboard buildings made by Pioneer Valley Models. To create a

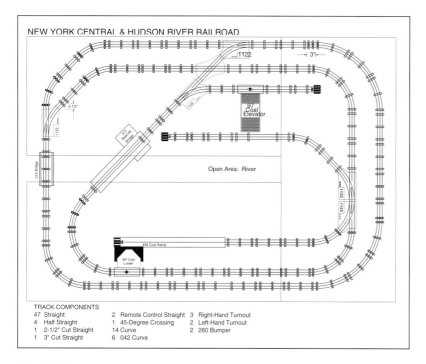

**Fig. 6-19**

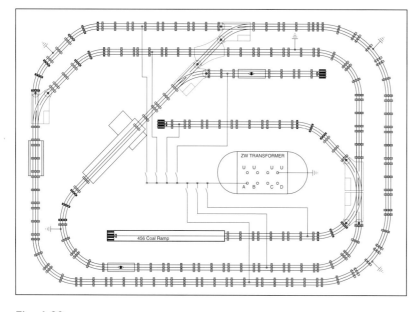

**Fig. 6-20**

convincing scene, you also must include streets, such as those made by Moondog Enterprises, and blocks of commercial buildings. (These and other addresses appear in Chapter 8.)

I built the elevated line (el) using 37 of Lionel's 111 trestles. They were sold in sets of ten between 1956 and 1969 and have been reissued as no. 2755. I relied on regular O27 curves and built elevated stations to accommodate the passengers. (Look for pictures of Chicago's

elevated line for structure ideas.) If you don't want to build stations for the elevated line, substitute 157 platforms. Don't forget stairs so your passengers can reach the el from street level.

For motive power, try a single 60 trolley. You can also use a tank-style or Dockside locomotive, such as Lionel's 8209, pulling and pushing a single coach, as seen in turn-of-the-century New York photos. For a more modern appearance, use a Rail Diesel Car.

The wiring for this layout is simple and straightforward, with one throttle controlling the elevated line in a single block and the other feeding the two mainline blocks and three sidings (fig. 6-15). If you want to add automatic operation to the el, you'll also need an automatic stop station, such as Lionel's 132.

Wire the station to a short insulated block at each end of the el as shown in fig. 6-16. If you're using a 60 trolley, which reverses by striking its bumper against an obstruction at the end of the line, be sure to make this block very short (one track section would be fine). At normal speeds, the trolley coasts far enough to hit the 260 bumper at the end before the 132 station cuts off its voltage. When the power comes back on, the trolley heads off in the opposite direction.

For a Dockside engine or a Rail Diesel Car, you must make the block longer, as shown in the diagram. If your locomotive has a two-position E-unit, it will head off in the opposite direction as soon as power returns to the track. If, like the RDC, it has a three-position E-unit, it will be in neutral when the stop station cycles the current back on. However, the station will automatically interrupt the current again, and when it comes on the next time, the RDC will be in reverse.

Note that there are two connections through toggle switches to the short tracks at the end. This allows an operator to select automatic operation by the 132 station or to bypass the station and send current directly to the track for manual operation.

Depotronics Inc. manufactures a sophisticated electronic circuit that's ideal for a point-to-point elevated railroad such as this one. The circuit provides automatic reversing at each end of the line, along with momentary stops at several stations along the way.

## INTERURBAN RAPID TRANSIT

I designed the Inter-urban Rapid Transit (IRT) as a variation on the Metropolitan Transit plan, but with O42 curves to accommodate Rail Diesel Cars on the elevated line. It's an out-and-back design, with the car leaving from and returning to the same spur siding shown at the bottom of fig. 6-17. Because the O42 turnout has an automatic non-derailing feature, the car reverses its direction around the loop every time it leaves the station.

The conventional lower-level railroad plan is a loop with a complex passing siding (disguised by the use of a 45-degree crossing) and

a single spur siding. This leaves plenty of room for urban buildings and scenery. The wiring system resembles that of the Metropolitan Transit layout, with one throttle for the lower level (through five blocks) and the

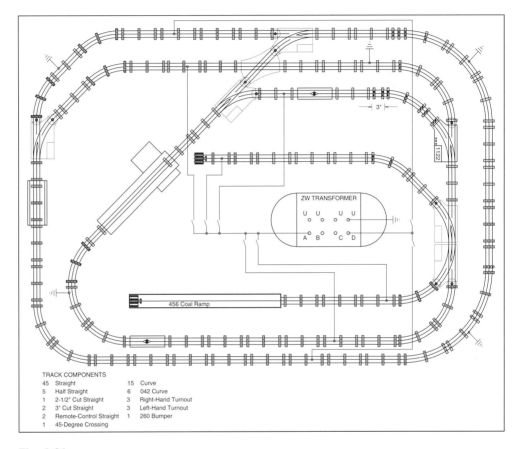

TRACK COMPONENTS

| | | | |
|---|---|---|---|
| 45 | Straight | 15 | Curve |
| 5 | Half Straight | 6 | 042 Curve |
| 1 | 2-1/2" Cut Straight | 3 | Right-Hand Turnout |
| 2 | 3" Cut Straight | 3 | Left-Hand Turnout |
| 2 | Remote-Control Straight | 1 | 260 Bumper |
| 1 | 45-Degree Crossing | | |

**Fig. 6-21**

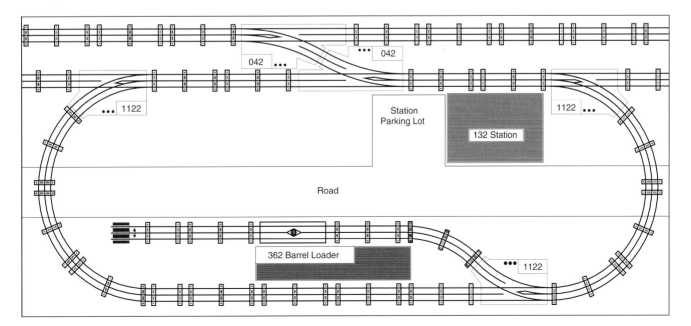

**Fig. 6-22**

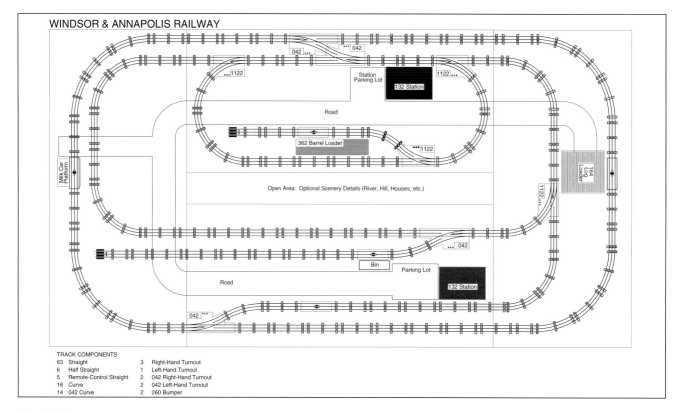

WINDSOR & ANNAPOLIS RAILWAY

TRACK COMPONENTS

| | | | |
|---|---|---|---|
| 63 | Straight | 3 | Right-Hand Turnout |
| 6 | Half Straight | 1 | Left-Hand Turnout |
| 5 | Remote-Control Straight | 2 | 042 Right-Hand Turnout |
| 16 | Curve | 2 | 042 Left-Hand Turnout |
| 14 | 042 Curve | 2 | 260 Bumper |

Fig. 6-23

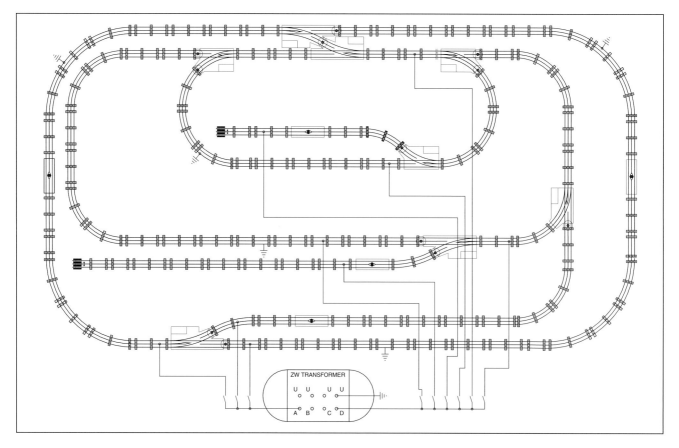

Fig. 6-24

other for the el (fig. 6-18). An operator may, through the toggles switches, select manual or automatic operation of the el. Or he or she can use a Depotronics circuit to provide automatic reversing and intermediate station stops.

## NEW YORK CENTRAL & HUDSON RIVER RAILROAD

In each of the foregoing designs all three tables are connected together, which leaves a convenient area for a control panel at one end. If you separate the two lengthwise tables as shown in fig. 6-19, you sacrifice the control panel area but gain a ready-made opening for a river.

Two bridges cross the river in this NYC&HRR concept: a simple girder bridge and Lionel's magnificent 313 bascule bridge. The perimeter is bound by a continuous loop, and the turnouts at top center and upper left provide a side trip, via the 45-degree crossing. Three sidings lend themselves to industries, such as the coal-loading accessories shown.

You can connect the entire layout to a single throttle (fig. 6-20), since there's only one continuous loop. Or, you can wire the outer loop to throttle A and all the inner tracks to throttle D. This would allow a train to

circle the perimeter while independent switching operations are carried out in the middle.

If you want to have two continuous loops, you can connect the uppermost stub siding at its right-hand end as shown in fig. 6-21. Using the two throttles as shown is the most logical way to proceed because it allows continuous independent running on both loops.

## WINDSOR & ANNAPOLIS RAILWAY

An island layout must allow access for the operator and viewers, and most average size rooms will probably not accommodate more than three or four tables. The Windsor & Annapolis Railway (named after a nine-teenth-century predecessor of Atlantic Canada's Intercolonial Railway) measures 12'8" by 6'8" and is probably the largest practical design for a spare room layout.

The heart of the layout is a small loop located entirely on one table (fig. 6-22). A builder can design it in modular fashion (see Chapter 5) for easy removal, in case he or she wishes to take it to a train meet to display it in a location away from home. There's room for a station, an industry, and a couple of additional buildings.

When inserted in the overall layout (fig. 6-23), the core table is part of a larger internal loop and connects

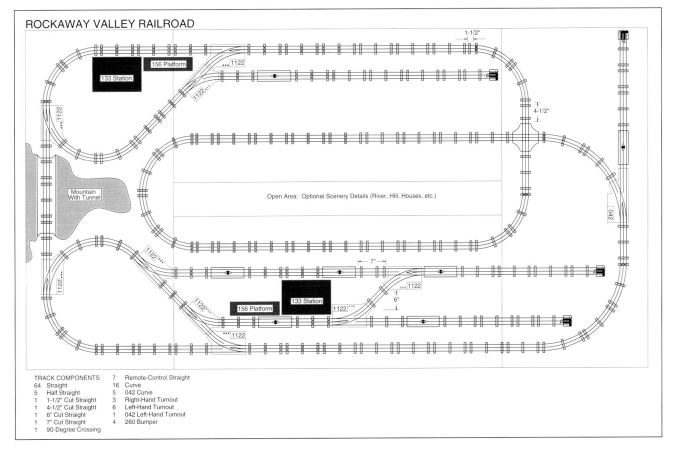

**Fig. 6-25**

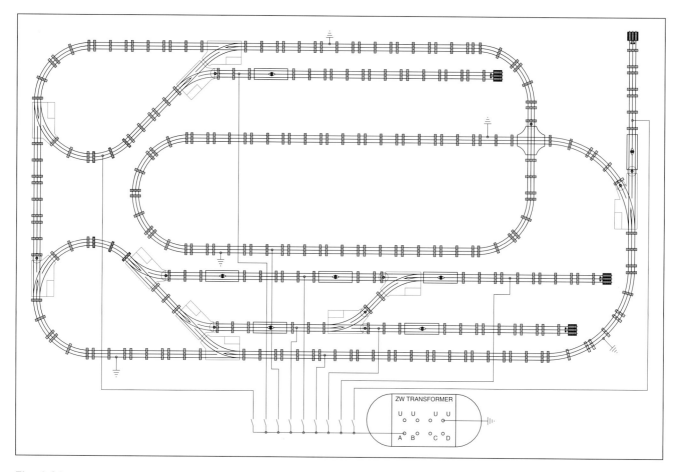

**Fig. 6-26**

to the perimeter loop through a crossover made from two O42 turnouts (top center). There's plenty of room for scenery and accessories, and the track geometry provides the correct spacing for a 97 coal loader or 164 log loader (right). The broad O42 curves on the outer loop accommodate even such large locomotives as Lionel's T-1 models.

Figure 6-24 shows a two-throttle system of wiring; it allows independent operation on two loops. On such a large layout, you should use heavy-gauge wire (14- or 12-gauge) for all track connections in order to reduce voltage drop.

## ROCKAWAY VALLEY RAILROAD

Residents of northern New Jersey may recognize this short line that briefly served the area between Whitehouse and Watnong in Hunterdon, Somerset, and Morris Counties around the turn of the century. People

nicknamed this train the "Rockabye Baby" because of its poorly ballasted and somewhat uneven trackwork. Traces of the right-of-way still can be found in the back woods.

My interpretation of the Rockaway Valley (fig. 6-25) is a false point-to-point layout, with a reverse loop at each end. You could eliminate the escape route through the tunnel at the left, giving a true point-to-point design, with Whitehouse at one reverse loop and Watnong at the other, and a long run between them. Instead of crowding the layout with a lot of track, the open areas offer opportunities for building scenery and adding accessories.

A simple one-throttle wiring pattern appears in fig. 6-26, but you could use two throttles instead. As with the previous design, use heavy-gauge wire, especially for connections to distant points.

In the next chapter we explore the techniques used to turn a track plan into a functional layout.

# 7

# LAYOUT MODIFICATION AND CONSTRUCTION

Rarely does an experienced modeler follow a published track plan exactly. The availability of differing accessories, buildings, or types of rolling stock may suggest altering or adapting a plan in any number of small ways. Such variations add individuality to a modeler's efforts. This chapter delineates basic techniques for building a sturdy structure for your layout so that the result, as the photos show, reflects departures from the chosen track plan.

The layout incorporates most of the principles that I've described in previous chapters. Its lightweight, modular design allows for easy portability and provides for a variety of interesting operational schemes, including the running of two or more trains at one time and using a number of representative Lionel accessories.

The track plan is a variation on the Berwick & Black Rock Railroad, which, as explained in Chapter 5, I designed to use sectional O27 trackage. In this incarnation, adapted for GarGraves flexible track, it has a less symmetrical appearance.

## OVERVIEW OF THE TRACK PLAN

The goal of the track plan is to provide an operator with maximum action in minimum space, giving a variety of routes over which the trains can travel. The two outer tables each contain a complete loop of track and therefore allow for continuous running. I've incorporated a reverse loop into each of these loops. The middle table also contains a reverse loop. There are two storage sidings, and a catenary system provides independent control of a second locomotive over the main line. An independent elevated passenger line adds more action.

The following diagrams show a simplified schematic of the layout, illustrating the six main travel routes. For clarity, I have omitted the point-to-point elevated line from these diagrams.

• A train can encircle the right-hand loop or the left-hand loop (fig. 7-1).

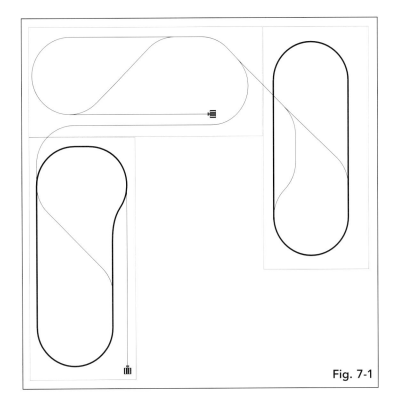

Fig. 7-1

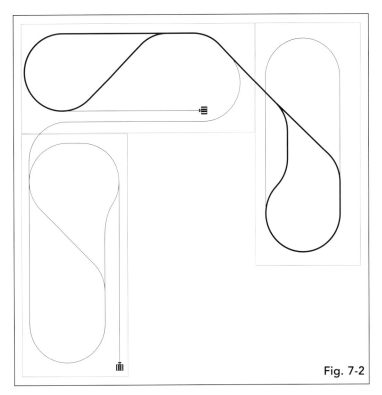

Fig. 7-2

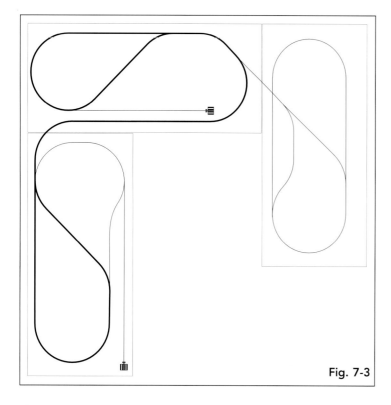

**Fig. 7-3**

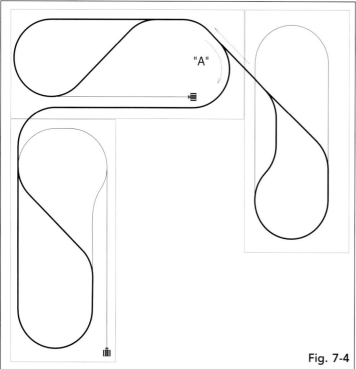

**Fig. 7-4**

• A train can travel continuously back and forth between the left-hand reverse loop and the middle table's reverse loop. No operator intervention is required, as nonderailing turnouts direct the train. With each repetition of the route, the train travels in the opposite direction through each of the reverse loops (fig. 7-3).

• A train can travel from the right-hand reverse loop, through the reverse loop on the middle table, then be directed through the turnout at "A" on the middle table toward the left-hand reverse loop, and then return. An operator need only change one turnout each time the train passes to maintain continuous operation (fig. 7-4).

• A passenger train can travel between the three station platforms on the elevated line, visible in the accompanying photographs.

Various accessories (also visible in the photographs) provide lots of action along the main line. This allows a modeler to operate them without having to divert trains from the main line. I've placed only one accessory, the 362 barrel loader, next to a siding on the middle table. To maximize operation, most of the layout has a simple catenary system. Two trains can operate continuously under independent control, one from middle-rail track power and one from the catenary.

The layout also features passenger service on the elevated line. If you use Rail Diesel Cars there, you must control them manually. As an alternative, you could run a Lionel 60 trolley continuously without operator supervision, as it will reverse itself automatically every time it strikes a bumper at the end of the line.

This layout favors smaller locomotives and rolling stock, appropriate to the relatively sharp curves, small buildings, and closely spaced scenic items. The use of 1121 and 1122 turnouts precludes running such items as Train Master diesel locomotives and large aluminum passenger cars. Instead, I recommend Alco diesels and NW2 switchers as the ideal motive power. GP7s and GP9s look all right, but any engine as large as an F3 tends to overwhelm the scenery.

## MATERIALS AND COMPONENTS

To keep costs to a reasonable level, I used turnouts and other components on hand instead of buying new ones. My wife and I have acquired these items over the

• A train can travel continuously back and forth between the right-hand reverse loop and the middle table's reverse loop. No operator intervention is required, as nonderailing turnouts direct the train. With each repetition of the route, the train travels in the opposite direction through each of the reverse loops (fig. 7-2).

years as we've accumulated used train sets. This amalgamation of components is most obvious in the wide variety of turnouts, including 022, 1121, 1122, 5132, and 5133 models as well as wide-radius O42 types (nos. 5167 and 5168). There are also different types of remote-control track sections, such as Lionel's UCS, 1019, and 6019 as well as GarGraves's uncouple/unload ramp and magnetic uncouplers. (A list of the items used appears at the end of the chapter.)

Two main differences are apparent when considering the mix of track used: the height of the railhead and the diameter of the tubular rail. The O gauge components (022, 5131, and 5132 turnouts and UCS ramps) are about ¼" higher than O27 or GarGraves components, and their track pins are thicker. The latter problem is easy to solve when using flexible track, since GarGraves markets two sizes of track pins that allow its track to mate with both O27 and O gauge track. If you're using sectional track, you can join O gauge to O27 by squeezing its rail ends to fit around the smaller O27 pins. Hobby shops carry special pliers that do this neatly.

You can easily accommodate the differing heights of O gauge and Lionel O27 or GarGraves track. I recommend either shimming up the O27 track with ¼" plywood or installing cork roadbed underneath all the GarGraves and O27 track and omitting it under the O gauge. I used the second method for the layout in this chapter.

## TABLE CONSTRUCTION

I first assembled the three tables, each of which is a 36"-wide hollow-core door supported by folding legs.

These doors owe their light weight to the thin construction of their surfaces, which are little more than veneer. The core of each door is made from a cardboard latticework grid; only the perimeter of the door is solid wood, and these wood strips are quite narrow, except on the side intended for the hinges. You can't attach the folding legs directly to the center areas of the doors, since the mounting screws will tear out of the veneer.

Cut two lengths of 1 x 3 spruce or pine for each end of each door, one 36" long and one about 14" long, to match the width of the mounting brackets on the folding legs (fig. 7-5). Screw the shorter length to the end of the door; the longer one bridges the distance between the edges of the door. Measure carefully to ensure

Fig. 7-6. In this top view, the ends of two pair of L-angles are visible as they project from the underside of the tables. As you slide the tables together, these angles guide them into alignment.

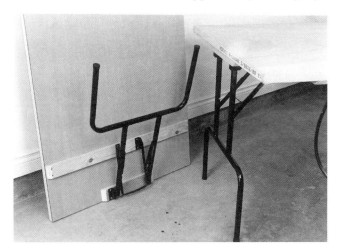

Fig. 7-5. These lightweight folding legs nicely support the train table but fold flat for easy portability. Secure each folding-leg assembly to the table with 1 x 3 pine strips. Screw the shorter strip to the end of the door, then attach the longer strip at its ends to both sides of the door.

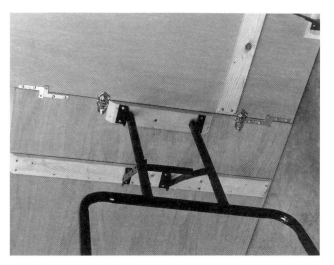

Fig. 7-7. The long legs of the L-angles are screwed to the edges of the table, while the short legs aren't screwed down. Inboard of the angles are two luggage catches, which hold the tables together.

Fig. 7-8. To be sure the plan works, test-fit all track components before making any permanent installation.

that you locate them correctly to match the dimensions of the legs.

Attach the wood strips using 1³/₄" x #8 wood screws. On the shorter end strip, you need to drive the screws through the holes in the folding leg bracket, through the pine, and into the door. For maximum strength, run a bead of carpenter's glue along the pine strips to hold them securely against the surface of the door.

If you are building the layout in a permanent location, fasten the tables together with L-or T-shaped metal angles screwed into the edge strips of the door. The layout pictured here is portable, with the tables joined in the following manner. Using a bolt cutter, shorten one leg on each L-angle and then screw the L-angles to one table edge. Fasten two similar angles to the adjoining table, so the first two angles enclose the short legs. When you push the two tables together, these angles ensure that the tables are always joined at the same location (fig. 7-6).

To hold the tables securely together, mount two luggage catches as shown in fig. 7-7. These catches keep the edges of the tables butted together tightly during operation.

## DETERMINING THE TRACK PLAN

When all three tables are joined, lay out the track components according to the plan you have chosen. If you're using sectional track, be sure to assemble it tightly. Test it with a variety of locomotives and rolling stock to be certain the plan works well and is exactly what you want. Remember to allow extra clearance around accessories located near the outside of curves. Many Lionel locomotives and such rolling stock as aluminum passenger cars have a considerable amount of overhang at the ends and will strike objects placed too near the track.

Make any changes in the plan now, before you start to install the track. When everything is arranged to your satisfaction, make a diagram so you'll be able to install various items correctly once you've painted the tables. (If you are using cork roadbed for this project, outline the track on the tables with a felt-tip marker and proceed as described below.)

Lay out the track as shown in fig. 7-8. Even if you build the final layout with flexible track on cork roadbed, you will find it easiest to use sectional curves to approximate the final design. Don't cut the flexible track; just lay it out in the estimated correct locations. When the plan meets your satisfaction, draw the center line of all the track components on the tables. This will require some careful measuring.

Start by laying out the curves. You can make a simple compass out of a wooden yardstick. Drill a small hole in

Fig. 7-9. As a guide for placing the cork roadbed, draw the locations of track components and accessories directly on the table with a felt-tip marker.

Fig. 7-10. Studying the eventual layout design is easier if you temporarily place all the accessories and buildings. Examine all lines of sight to be sure that operating accessories and other attractive components aren't hidden from view. Pay particular attention to the clearance between accessories and track.

Fig. 7-11. Install strips of roadbed in two halves along the track center lines on the table. Note that there is no roadbed under the O gauge turnouts because they are higher than the track to be attached to them. In the foreground strips of roadbed support an O27 turnout, which is the same height as the flexible track.

the yardstick at the 1" mark, equidistant from the edges. This will serve as the pivot point. Next, determine the radius of the curve you wish to draw. For example, if you want a 30"-diameter curve, the radius will be 15". Drill another small hole in the yardstick at the 16" location (*not* the 15" position; because the pivot point is at the 1" mark, a 15" radius will be at the 16" position.)

Then determine the center point of the curve, and use a small finishing nail to anchor the pivot point of the yardstick. Place another finishing nail in the hole at the 16" position, and rotate the yardstick to inscribe the center line of the curve directly on the table. (Remember that you measure the diameter of Lionel sectional track over the *outside* and not the center rail. A curve with a 15"-radius *center* line measures about $31^1/4$" over the diameter of the *outside* rail, or a little larger than O gauge sectional track.)

You can lay out all the curves in this manner, no matter what radius you have chosen. Just drill a hole in the yardstick at the appropriate distance from the pivot point. As you become more experienced, you will find that easement curves (those that are less severely curved at the beginning and end than in the middle) look more realistic and provide for better operation. Be sure, however, not to make any curves tighter than a diameter of 27" (13"-radius center line).

When you've located all the curves, reinforce the scored center lines with a felt-tip marker to make them more visible. Then mark the straight sections of track with the marker (fig. 7-9), according to your track plan. Be sure to use an accurate straightedge, such as a steel carpenter's rule; wooden yardsticks are seldom absolutely straight. After you've completed the diagram, examine it for accuracy by comparing it with the plan.

Next, position all of your accessories and buildings on the table to be sure they fit. Remember that the markings for the track are of its center line, and make sure that nothing is closer to it than 2". You may wish to leave the track plan in place to make it easier to visualize the final layout (fig. 7-10). When everything is located to your satisfaction, make a diagram for future reference. You may also want to write the name and location of each accessory directly on the table (fig. 7-9); you'll later cover these markings with paint. The *best* way to record the locations of items is to take photographs of their temporary placement. Don't trust your memory!

Fig. 7-12. Sprayed-on speckle-stone paint successfully imitates a gravel roadbed without the chore of spreading and gluing loose ballast.

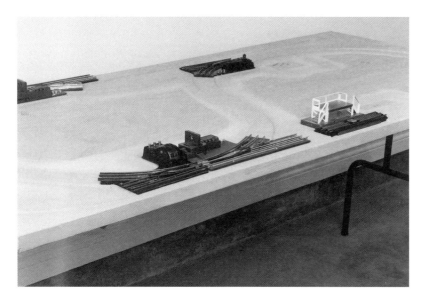

Fig. 7-13. Before cutting any flexible track, lay out the sectional pieces (turnouts, remote-control sections, and crossings) in their proper locations.

## INSTALLING THE ROADBED

If all the track is the same height, mount the cork roadbed along all the center lines you've drawn on the table. If some of the track is higher, such as the O gauge turnouts combined with flexible track in this layout, put the higher components accurately in place and install the roadbed around them. Remember that O27 track on cork roadbed will be the same height as O gauge track mounted directly on the table.

Cork roadbed is sold in 36" strips, and each strip comes in two halves, with beveled edges. Use contact cement to fasten it; doing so eliminates the need to

clamp the roadbed in place while it dries. Start by coating the back of the roadbed with a thin layer of cement. While this dries, spread cement on the table along the center line of the track, approximately as wide as the roadbed. Because the roadbed is porous, I recommend applying a second coat of cement after the first coat has set up (about five minutes). A second coat isn't needed on the table.

When the cement on both the roadbed and the table is dry to the touch (this takes about ten minutes), carefully align the *straight* edge of one of the half strips along the center line. The *beveled* edge goes on the outside. Be sure the roadbed is exactly in position before you allow contact between it and the table; once the cement bonds, separating the roadbed from the table is very difficult.

Next, place the other half strip of roadbed along the opposite side of the center line (fig. 7-11). Be sure the two half strips butt together tightly in the center. Using a small block of wood, tap the roadbed along its entire length to secure the bond. Then continue on to the next strip. You can cut the roadbed to fit under turnouts and other odd-shaped components as shown in the photograph. Use a straightedge and a hobby knife equipped with a sharp no. 11 blade in order to get a clean cut with no ragged edges.

You may wish to apply ballast after installing the track, but I prefer to *imitate* ballast by painting the roadbed with a simulated speckle-stone paint, available in spray cans. This paint is easier and far less messy to apply than loose ballast. For a portable layout such as this one, you'll want to avoid using fragile scenic materials that may come loose.

Cork roadbed comes in a variegated brown color, so you can use it without having to paint it, although the color may not correspond to your concept of ballast. If not, choose a color that you like. I picked a dirty tan; Nova Scotia ballast is mostly dirt and gravel. Several shades of gray are also available. You'll need both the speckle-stone paint and a quart of flat latex base coat in approximately the same color.

First paint the roadbed with the flat latex paint. Also paint an area of the table around the roadbed at least 1"

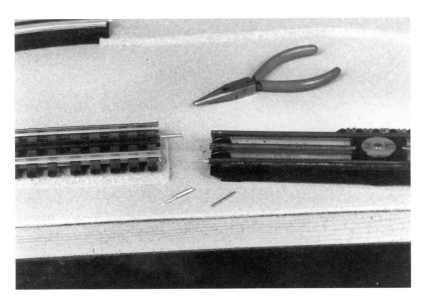

Fig. 7-14. Ordinary GarGraves track pins (right foreground) are too thin to use when joining flexible track to Lionel track. You must use special pins that are thin on one end and thick on the other (left foreground). Two of these pins are also shown inserted in the track, the thin end in the GarGraves rail (left) and the thick end in a Lionel UCS track section (right).

use a 224 locomotive and rolling stock from Lionel's first postwar set, 463W from 1945. The flying shoe couplers used in this set are susceptible to catching on uneven track. If this train works properly over your layout, you can expect most others probably will, too.)

If you are using GarGraves flexible track, bend and cut it according to the instructions provided by the manufacturer. (An excellent article on laying Gar-Graves track appears in *Classic Toy Trains* magazine, November 1996.) Test each section for smoothness as you install it, and be sure there are no kinks in the rail. GarGraves makes pins in both O27 and O gauge sizes for joining its rail to Lionel components (fig. 7-14).

Adjust each joint until there is an absolutely smooth transition between each section (fig. 7-15). Extra time spent here prevents considerable annoyance later, as flexible track is difficult to adjust once the entire layout is in place.

Use ³/₄" x #4 flathead wood screws to secure the flexible track to the table. Drill holes in the wood ties first; they'll split if you try to drive screws through them directly. On straight sections, using one screw for every tenth tie is usually sufficient, but on curves and where sections of track meet, you should use enough screws to ensure absolute stability and permanence. (The Gar-Graves instruction sheet offers additional hints for

on either side. If there will be areas of the layout where you want to simulate dirt, paint those areas as well. One coat is sufficient, and it need not cover completely. After this base coat has dried, spray the area with the speckle-stone paint (fig. 7-12). I advise doing this outdoors on a windless day, as the paint has a strong odor and releases a good amount of residue into the air. A heavy coat gives the most realistic simulation of ballast.

## LAYING THE TRACK

When the paint has dried completely, begin laying the track by locating the turnouts and remote-control sections in their proper locations (fig. 7-13). I also installed the platform for the automatic milk car at this time, as the remote-control track section rests on top of it. Temporarily screw these components in place.

If you are using sectional track, assemble the sections and join them to the turnouts and remote-control tracks. Remember to use fiber or plastic insulating track pins wherever you want to isolate a block or an outside insulated rail for controlling accessories. Adjust all sections until they fit properly on the roadbed, and ensure that all joints are tight. Then test them with your most sensitive locomotive and rolling stock. (I

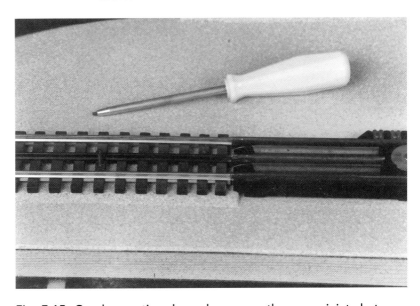

Fig. 7-15. Good operation depends on smooth, secure joints between the track sections.

installation; you may also wish to consult *Tips and Tricks for Toy Train Operators,* listed in Chapter 8.)

When you have completed one section of track (a loop, for example), test it thoroughly and carefully to be sure that there are no kinks or rough joints (fig. 7-16). I recommend completing *all* the track work before adding any scenery or accessories, as there often are rough spots for you to work out. When everything is operating to your satisfaction, temporarily lay out the accessories and such scenic elements as roads, according to your plan.

Remember that the larger Lionel locomotives and cars have a considerable amount of overhang on sharp curves. Anything located near the *outside edge* of a curve should be placed far enough from the track for adequate clearance. Test each accessory location with your largest equipment. Also watch for clearance problems on the *inside* of curves, where long locomotives and passenger cars may strike objects placed too near the track.

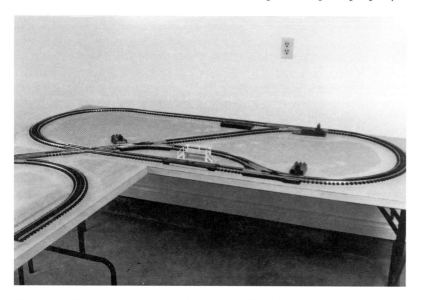

Fig. 7-16. Once you've installed a loop of flexible track, visualizing the appearance of the final layout becomes easier.

Fig. 7-17. Moondog streets are rubber-based imitation asphalt, with center lines and other markings in place. Each set includes a variety of shapes and sizes, all of which are easily cut to size.

## INSTALLING THE HIGHWAY SYSTEM

If you are using Moondog streets, I suggest cutting and fitting them at this time (fig. 7-17). Locate them properly in relation to all accessories, especially crossing gates and buildings, and secure them to the table with white glue. These roads lie flat and require only a few drops of glue on the back of each section. This allows for easier removal when you decide to change the layout. These road sections, which have a thickness of $\frac{1}{4}$", will lie unrealistically on top of the table at this point. This will not be a problem when the rest of the scenery is added.

Figure 7-18 shows various accessories and buildings, including the 362 barrel loader, 394 rotary beacon, 450 signal bridge, 464 sawmill, and 3356 horse corral (partially visible behind and to the left of the sawmill). Install and test the operation of those accessories that you plan to fasten directly to the table. Others, such as the beacon and the houses, will be attached to other parts of the scenery. As a result, you shouldn't fasten them permanently yet. Test all clearances after you've installed every item.

## NEAT AND FUNCTIONAL WIRING

Newcomers to this hobby are frequently surprised at how much wiring even a modest Lionel layout requires. By the time you connect track blocks, turnouts, remote-control tracks, accessories, and lights, the number of connections can easily reach the hundreds. Plan your wiring scheme carefully, so that when repairs and maintenance are needed, it will be easy to trace the connections. A detailed discussion of layout wiring is beyond the scope of this book (see Chapter 8 for some recommended

Fig. 7-18. When all the roads are in place, temporarily locate each accessory you plan to use on your layout. Check clearances with your largest pieces of equipment. If any changes in the roads are necessary, make them now.

hollow-core door can be tricky. Drill a small hole all the way through the table and then increase the size of the hole on the underside with a larger drill bit. Also put a lamp under the table when feeding wires down through the hole. The light shining up through the hole makes it easier to find.

• The appearance of your layout will not benefit from the use of Lionel lockons for track wiring. Instead, force the end of a track wire into the slot on the underside of the rail. For extra permanence and more positive electrical contact, solder it in place. Then drill a hole in the table directly under the rail and feed the wire through. It will be nearly invisible when the track is installed.

guides), but these basic principles should usually apply.

• Color-code your wiring. Use a different color for each function, such as red for track power, green for accessories, yellow for lights, and so forth. You can make repairs more rapidly if you can easily trace individual wires.

• Use common-ground wiring. Run a ground loop around the entire layout, and ground every track block, accessory, and light to it. Then you'll need only one power wire for each component, an arrangement that saves a lot of wire. (The first volume of *Wiring Your Lionel Layout* contains a discussion of common-ground wiring.)

• Use heavy-gauge wire for track power (16- or 14-gauge), and connect each block of track at two or more locations. Voltage drop is a problem with sectional track, since the track pins tend to loosen over time. If your trains slow down at certain points on the layout, run additional wires to those points.

• Connect only *one* wire to each transformer post and then connect them to a terminal strip. Use more terminal strips to distribute power to the layout (fig. 7-19). This arrangement makes disconnecting a transformer much easier if it needs repair or replacement.

• On portable or modular layouts, use quick-disconnect plugs between tables (fig. 7-20); these parts are available from any electronics supply store.

• Wherever possible, use mechanical rather than soldered connections. Inexpensive connectors, such as those in fig. 7-20, simplify making changes and removing items from the layout for repair.

• Feeding a wire through a layout table made from a

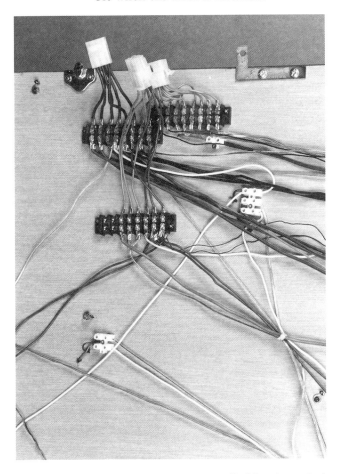

Fig. 7-19. Terminal strips (sometimes called barrier strips) consist of hard plastic bars fitted with pairs of screw-type wire attachment points. Those shown here contain eight pairs each; smaller and larger strips are available, containing as few as two to as many as twenty pairs. Using these strips greatly simplifies repairs and revisions to the wiring system.

## TRANSFORMER LOCATION

You can locate transformers directly on the layout, but they steal valuable space. Instead, make a removable transformer table (especially useful for portable layouts) from a short length of 1 x 6 pine or from a prefinished shelf such as the one shown in fig. 7-21. I mounted the shelf on two U-shaped channels that slide into brackets under the table.

Run the wires from each transformer through a quick-disconnect plug to a terminal strip under the layout. If you plan to move the layout, you'll be able to slide the entire transformer table out of its brackets to transport separately. For neatness and easy troubleshooting, group all wires wherever possible with nylon cable ties (fig. 7-22) from electronics or auto supply stores.

## ACCESSORIES

Install the wiring for each operating accessory before you begin work on the scenery. Most Lionel accessories require just two connections: one wire to the common ground and the other to the transformer through a push button or a slide switch that Lionel provides. You may substitute a toggle switch. Follow the instructions packed with the accessory.

Next, connect the automatic accessories to fixed-voltage posts and insulated rails or electronic sensors. Test each item as you install it, and be sure it works properly before proceeding to the next one. In fact, I recommend testing *every* installation immediately after it is complete. Run the trains to be sure that clearances are adequate, and check that each circuit performs properly. You'll find that debugging a layout is much easier *before* you've added the scenery.

## MODULAR SCENERY

There are many different methods of making model railroad scenery, and a wide variety of books can be found in hobby shops. The method you choose depends in part on the degree of realism you wish to achieve. For this project, I chose to capture the toy train look pioneered by Lionel in the years between the First and Second World Wars.

During the Depression, Lionel marketed its line of small houses both individually and as components in a system of modular scenic plots. The smallest of these

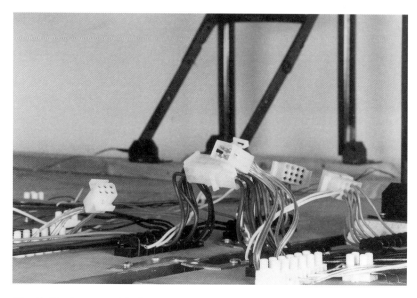

Fig. 7-20. On portable layouts or those with tables that may have to be moved, you can make wire connections with quick-disconnect plugs, available from electronics supply houses. They provide secure contact with little resistance and are shaped so they cannot be mated incorrectly. They come in various sizes, to accommodate as few as two or as many as twelve wires.

Fig. 7-21. The transformer table reveals its supports when pulled away from the layout. When I have to move the layout, I can slide this table out farther and completely remove it for travel. Wire connections are made through quick-disconnect plugs.

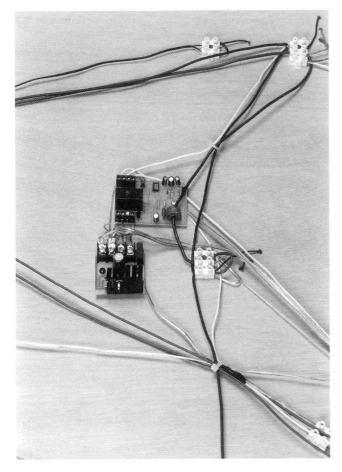

Fig. 7-22. Beneath the table, wires are gathered together and held taut by nylon cable ties. This provides a neat appearance and avoids the danger of slack or dangling wires when the layout is moved.

Fig. 7-23. A paper pattern allows the builder to transfer the shape of a scenic area to a piece of ¹/₄" plywood prior to cutting it out. Here are several plywood plots beneath the houses and resting on the track in front of the Lionel 46 crossing gate.

consisted of a single house set on a ¹/₄" base made of composite board and decorated with grass, hedges, flowers, and trees. More elaborate versions had multiple houses, roadways, lampposts, and parks.

You can easily duplicate this method for a toy train layout. Make a paper pattern for each area where a scenic plot is to be located (fig. 7-23). Allow ¹/₄" clearance between the edge of a plot and the rail line roadbed. This will simulate a ditch. Where the plots abut highways and other scenic items, be sure to make the pattern as accurate as possible.

Quarter-inch plywood faced with poplar, available in 4-foot-square sheets, makes a good surface for a scenic plot (fig. 7-24). Turn the plywood so the good face is downward. Then turn the plywood pattern face down, and secure it to the plywood with masking tape. Using a handheld jigsaw or saber saw, cut out the plot by following the paper pattern. (Because the saw cuts on the *up stroke*, cutting with the good side of the wood downward gives the cleanest cut.)

Cut at a 90-degree angle for edges of the plot that meet other scenic elements. Set the blade at 45 degrees for sloped edges, such as those forming the ditch along a rail line. Then, using a small block plane, shape the beveled edges and sand the entire plot. Rough sanding is sufficient, as you don't need a perfectly smooth finish; scenic elements will cover the surface.

Test the plot on the layout, and use the plane and sandpaper to achieve the best fit. Next determine the scenic elements to be installed on the plot. If you plan on adding structures, locate and mark their foundations on the plot. The Greenleaf Village houses I used don't have foundations, so I made them from stripwood and glued them to the scenic plots (fig. 7-24).

Now you must decide where to locate such elements as sidewalks, driveways, and pathways, and paint those areas in appropriate colors: gray for asphalt, light beige for cement, etc. For a textured appearance, overspray with speckle-stone paint in matching colors (fig. 7-25).

Once the paint has dried thoroughly, mask off all areas you want to protect. Then apply a coat of green paint to those areas that form the basis for grass. Use two coats to seal the surface completely. Then apply a thick third coat, working with one small section at a time, and sprinkle on your choice of grass or

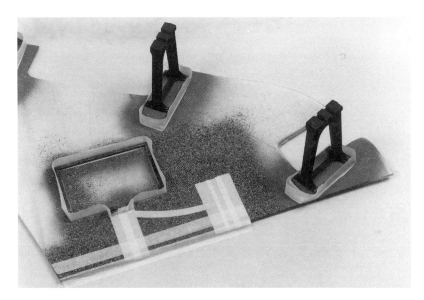

Fig. 7-24. I've installed towers for the elevated line and a house foundation on this scenic plot, cut from ¼" plywood. Applying masking tape allows a builder to spray-paint selected areas of the plot, in this case an imitation asphalt parking area around a schoolhouse. Dark gray speckle-stone paint makes excellent pavement.

Fig. 7-25. This scenic plot, with house foundation and sidewalk areas already spray-painted, is installed abutting the Moondog road material. (Compare this view with fig. 7-26.)

ground cover. Using a small flat block of wood, press the grass firmly down into the paint and let it dry. Then shake off any excess.

Install the plots on the layout with contact cement or small flathead screws (fig. 7-26). If you use screws, paint their tops green and cover them with grass mixture. Place the buildings on their foundations and secure them with screws from inside. Drill a hole through the floor of each building, scenic plot, and

train table for the interior lighting wires. Add lamp posts, landscaping (trees, hedges, and so forth), and details such as fire plugs, dogs and cats, and people.

Choose relatively low-voltage transformer posts to power the lamp posts and buildings, as a soft glow is more realistic than a harsh, bright one. Most of the bulbs on this layout are rated at 14 volts, and I used the 11-volt posts of a 1033 transformer. If you have a lot of lights, consider using a separate transformer to avoid overloading.

## ELEVATED LINE

If you are planning an elevated line, prepare for it *before* you paint the scenic plots. Consider raising the el higher than the less than 5" of overhead clearance provided by Lionel's trestle sets. I used 1 x 2 pine to make elevated supports for each trestle tower (called a "bent"), then cut them at a 45-degree angle at each end to simulate concrete piers (fig. 7-27). Determine where all the piers should go, and secure them to the scenic plots with flathead wood screws driven upward through the plywood panels.

Be careful when locating each pier, especially if you are using sectional track for the elevated line. Once you've installed the piers, you can't move them without disturbing the rest of the scenery. Spray the piers with textured speckle-stone paint at the same time you're painting the sidewalks and building foundations (fig. 7-24).

When all the scenic plots are in place on the layout, but before you complete the scenery, fasten the Lionel trestles to the piers with short (¹/₂" x #4) roundhead screws. Install the track, wire it to a transformer, and test it for smooth operation.

Lionel's track, like that put out by GarGraves, is self-supporting when installed on these trestles, despite the fact that it looks as though the ties aren't supported (fig. 7-28). This is fine for a toylike appearance, but if you want it to seem more realistic, install stripwood stringers between the trestles so the ties appear to be held up by the stringers. Paint the stripwood before installation, and fasten it to the bottom of the ties with contact cement.

Lionel station platforms make good elevated terminals. You'll need some means for the passengers to ascend to the platform, such as open stairways. If you don't want to spend the time on this detail, put a painted block of wood between the platform and the ground level, and install double doors at the top and bottom to simulate an elevator or enclosed stairway.

## CATENARY SYSTEM

In order to run two trains simultaneously on this relatively small layout, I installed a catenary system over parts of the line for my collection of GG1 and EP-5 locomotives. Various suppliers market realistic catenary components, although the cost isn't low. I made the system shown in the photos from different sizes of music wire. It provides reliable operation and is durable and light in weight (important considerations on a portable layout). It doesn't exactly resemble prototype overhead wiring systems, but it does convey the *impression* quite well (fig. 7-29).

I used a second transformer (a 1033) to power the catenary line. Since it uses the same rails for a ground as the primary transformer (an LW), the two transformers must be *in phase* to work together. Consult a wiring text, such as *Greenberg's Wiring Your Lionel Layout*, Vol. II (listed in Chapter 8), for information about using multiple transformers on the same layout. (My method for building simple catenary systems appears in the November 1996 *Classic Toy Trains* magazine. I've outlined a simpler design in *Tips and Tricks for Toy Train Operators*.)

## A FEW FINAL WORDS

I have lost count of the number of layouts I have built over a lifetime of involvement in model railroading. In the category of toy trains alone, they number more than twenty. While I enjoy running Lionel trains, my greatest joy comes from building layouts, and I've experimented with many methods of construction. The foregoing method is a brief com-

Fig. 7-26. I've added grass to form lawns and to outline sidewalks and the driveway in front of the garage. Placing masking tape over the sidewalk keeps the grass from adhering in the wrong places. The rubber-based street material from Moondog is easy to cut and install, comes in a variety of straight and curved sections, and is printed with realistic traffic markings, including stop signs (shown) and railroad crossing warnings. If you don't use the Moondog product, consider painting roads directly on the scenic plots.

Fig. 7-27. I mounted each of the towers supporting the elevated line on a wood base to raise it to the desired level for clearance above the trains and scenery. Also visible are an uninstalled scenic plot (center), a milk platform in front of a remote-control section (left), a 450 signal bridge and a 46 crossing gate from Lionel (left and center), and a telltale post for operating the giraffe and elephant cars (between the gate and the signal bridge). The lamp post is an American Flyer product.

pilation of many ideas developed over the years, but is by no means conclusive (figs. 7-30 through 7-34).

If you're about to embark upon your first layout,

keep it simple. Each time you build a new layout it will be better, as you benefit from the skills you developed when building the previous one. And if you develop new techniques that will benefit the rest of us, please share your ideas. We'll be pleased to include them in future editions of this and other Kalmbach books. I invite your comments and suggestions, addressed to me at Kalmbach Books, Kalmbach Publishing Co., 21027 Crossroads Circle, P. O. Box 1612, Waukesha, WI 53187-1612.

Fig. 7-28. Lionel's 400 Budd Rail Diesel Car arrives to pick up passengers on the elevated line. The sturdy GarGraves track needs no support between trestles, although it would look more realistic with some support beams (stringers) installed. Note the passenger about to enter the elevator for a trip down to ground level!

Fig. 7-29. Catenary wires above the tracks add a pleasing urban appearance to a layout. On the elevated line, a Lionel 60 trolley trundles back and forth continually without operator assistance, thanks to its automatic reversing feature.

Fig. 7-30. Although featuring plentiful scenery, many accessories, and continuous three-train operation, this U-shaped portable layout fits easily into half a spare room. If located in a child's bedroom, it still leaves room for necessary furniture and affords storage space beneath.

Fig. 7-31. An engineer's-eye view shows a departing freight train and arriving Budd car at the right-hand end of the layout.

Fig. 7-33. Industries abound, giving the freight trains legitimate reasons for their travels. Here a conscientious Lionel worker loads kegs of a product from Nova Scotia's world-famous apple orchards for the Annapolis Valley Apple Cider Company (a 362 barrel loader).

Fig. 7-32. Although the trackwork is relatively complex, there is still room for trees, roads, automobiles, and buildings, all of which give the layout a feeling of bustling human activity.

Fig. 7-34. Passengers enjoy riding the elevated trolley, safe from the hazards of a military transport train (leased by this Canadian rail line from the mighty Santa Fe) on the tracks below.

## MATERIALS LIST

**Accessories and Transformers
(Lionel unless noted otherwise)**
Animal Car Track Trip
LW Transformer
Marx 25-watt Transformer
Right-Of-Way Highway Flasher
  Signals
025 Bumpers, 2
47 Crossing Gate
48W Whistle Station
127 Station
157 Station Platform
260 Bumpers, 2
362 Barrel Loader
450 Signal Bridges, 2
1033 Transformer
3356 Horse Car Corral
3462P Milk Car Platforms, 2
4150 Transformer
5906 Sound Activation Controls, 2
12731 Station Platforms, 2
12812 Freight/Passenger Station
12847 Icing Station
12862 Oil Drum Loader
12873 Operating Sawmill

**Lumber**
1" x 2" pine or spruce, 24 feet
1" x 3" pine or spruce, 20 feet
4'0" x 4'0" x ¹/₄" plywood faced
  with poplar one side, 2 sheets
3'0" x 6'8" hollow-core doors, 3
Folding table legs, 3 pairs

**Miscellaneous Hardware**
Assorted accessory switches

Double-pole double-throw
  knife switches
Music wire
Quick-disconnect plugs
Single-pole single-throw knife
  switches
Terminal strips
14-gauge hookup wire, 50 feet
16-gauge hookup wire, 25 feet
18-gauge hookup wire, 50 feet
20-gauge hookup wire, 50 feet

**Scenery Materials**
Greenleaf Village structures
Moondog Enterprises roads

**Track (Lionel unless noted
otherwise)**
GarGraves Magnetic Uncouplers, 3
GarGraves Phantom Sectional
  Track, 24 sections
GarGraves Uncouple/unload
  Ramp
O Gauge Insulated Track Pins
O27 Gauge Insulated Track Pins
Super O Gauge Insulated Track
  Pins
Transition Track Pins (GarGraves
  to O27 Gauge)
Transition Track Pins (GarGraves
  to O Gauge)
UCS O Gauge Remote-Control
  Tracks, 3
022 O Gauge Remote-Control
  Switches, 2
1019 O27 Remote-Control Track

1121 O27 Remote-Control Switches
1122 O27 Remote-Control
  Switches
5023 O27 45-Degree Crossing
5132 O Gauge Remote-Control
  Right-Hand Switch
5133 O Gauge Remote-Control
  Left-Hand Switch
5167 O42 Remote-Control
  Right-Hand Switches, 2
5168 O42 Remote-Control Left-
  Hand Switches, 2
6019 O27 Remote-Control Track

**Wood Screws**
¹/₂" x #4, flathead
¹/₂" x #4, roundhead
⁵/₈" x #6, roundhead
³/₄" x #4, flathead
³/₄" x #4, roundhead
1" x #4, roundhead
1³/₄" x #8

# 8

# REFERENCES

## BOOKS

Information supplementary to the topics discussed in this book appears in the following publications. Those still in print, indicated by an asterisk, can be ordered from Kalmbach Publishing Co., 1-800-533-6644; the other books, out of print at press time, may still be available at hobby stores or from used book dealers at swap meets or train shows.

Grams, John. *Beginner's Guide to Toy Train Collecting and Operating.*

Kouba, John. *Greenberg's Model Railroading with Lionel Trains, Vol. 2: An Advanced Layout.*

Lang, Cliff. *Greenberg's Layout Plans for Lionel Trains.*

LaVoie, Roland E. *Greenberg's Model Railroading with Lionel Trains.*

Plummer, Ray L. *Beginner's Guide to Repairing Lionel Trains* (available October 1997).

Riddle, Peter H. *Greenberg's Wiring Your Lionel Layout: A Primer for Lionel Train Enthusiasts.*

_____. *Greenberg's Wiring Your Lionel Layout, Vol. 2: Intermediate Techniques.*

_____. *Greenberg's Wiring Your Lionel Layout, Vol. 3: Advanced Technologies Made Easy.*

_____. *Tips and Tricks for Toy Train Operators.*

_____. *Trains from Grandfather's Attic.*

Trzoniec, Stanley W. *How to Build Your First Lionel Layout.*

## MANUFACTURERS AND SUPPLIERS

Materials applicable to the projects in this book are available from the following firms:

All-Trol Products, 37 Hurley Circle, Marlboro, MA 01752; 508-481-2238: power supplies.

Circuitron, P. O. Box 322, Riverside, IL 60546: electronic control devices.

Curtis High Rail Products Inc., P. O. Box 385, North Stonington, CT 06359; 1-800-227-7245: turnouts and sectional track products.

Dallee Electronics, 10 Witmer Rd., Lancaster, PA 17602; 717-392-1705: electronic control devices.

Depotronics, P. O. Box 2093, Warrendale, PA 15086; 412-776-4061: electronic control devices.

GarGraves Trackage Corp., 8967 Ridge Rd., North Rose, NY 14516-9793; 315-483-6577: turnouts and sectional track products.

Moondog Express, P. O. Box 1707, Lompoc, CA 93438; 805-733-1190: streets, ties, track patterns.

Oakridge Corp., P. O. Box 247, Lemont, IL 60439: Greenleaf Village and other buildings and landscape materials.

Pioneer Valley Models, P. O. Box 4928, Holyoke, MA 01041: backdrops and cardstock buildings.

Right-Of-Way Industries, P. O. Box 13036, Akron, OH 44313; 216-867-5361: turnouts, track products and signals.

Ross Custom Switches, P. O. Box 110, North Stonington, CT 06359; 1-800-331-1395: turnouts, sectional track products, automatic crossing gates.